W9-BPL-924

👁 INSIGHT COMPACT GUIDE

CAMBODIA

Compact Guide: Cambodia is the ideal quick-reference guide to this fabulous Southeast Asian destination. It tells you everything you need to know about Cambodia's attractions, from the palace and markets of Phnom Penh to the idyllic beaches, from the banks of the Mekong to the wonders of Angkor.

This is one of more than 133 Compact Guides, which combine the interests and enthusiasms of two of the world's best known information providers: Insight Guides, whose titles have set the standard for visual travel guides since 1970, and Discovery Channel, the world's premier source of nonfiction television programming.

Discovery
CHANNEL

APA PUBLICATIONS
Part of the Langenscheidt Publishing Group
L

Star Attractions

An instant reference to some of Cambodia's most popular attractions to help you set your priorities.

Royal Palace p23

Phnom Penh's markets p26

The Coast p36

Phnom Chisor p34

Angkor Thom p43

Bayon reliefs p44

Angkor Wat p47

Preah Khan p52

Tonlé Sap p65

Royal Ballet p73

Preah Vihear p68

Cambodia

Cambodia – Land of the God-Kings

Opposite: Royal Palace in Phnom Penh

For much of the late 20th century Cambodia has been synonymous with suffering. For around three decades the country's very name has conjured up images of internecine warfare, bombings, land mines and famine – and over it all has loomed the menacing shadow of the Khmer Rouge. Yet Cambodia was not always like this. Before being engulfed in the maelstrom of the Vietnam War during the late 1960s, the country had an enviable reputation as a land of peace and tranquillity. Literature of the time waxes lyrical about the beauty of the countryside, where a prosperous and contented people welcomed visitors who travelled half-way round the world to see the astonishing, wonderful temple complex of Angkor.

In the last decade, Cambodia, newly at peace, has struggled to rebuild itself in its old image. Today a great deal remains to be done, but considerable advances have been made. The last Khmer Rouge guerillas have surrendered or been captured. Land mines in the vicinity of Angkor and other major monuments have been cleared or cordoned off to make these areas safe for tourism – a business surely destined to become one of Cambodia's major foreign exchange earners in the near future as the country continues to open to visitors. For make no mistake, Angkor is *the* major historical attraction in Southeast Asia. In fact, nothing on earth exists to compare with the capital of the former Khmer *devaraja* or 'God-Kings', unless it is Egypt's Valley of the Nile.

Yet there is more to Cambodia than just Angkor. Other temple complexes are fast becoming accessible to visitors, including the isolated cliff-top temple of Preah Vihear. Besides temples, Phnom Penh – a verdant city of broad boulevards and riverside cafés set by the *Chatomuk*, or confluence of the Sap, Bassac and Mekong rivers – is slowly reassuming its old appeal. Then there is the southern coast, where the seaside resorts of Sihanoukville (Kompông Som) and even Kep – the latter completely destroyed as an act of 'class warfare' by the Khmer Rouge – offer wonderful opportunities for swimming, diving and other watersports.

At Phnom Penh's O Russei Market

Monks at Preah Vihear

Position and size

Almost twice the size of Portugal, but with a similar number of people, Cambodia is a relatively flat, low-lying land. Situated at the heart of Indochina, it has a total area of just over 180,000sq km (69,500sq miles). It shares land borders with Laos to the northeast, Vietnam to the east and southeast, and Thailand to the north and west. In addition, Cambodia has a 443-km (277-mile)

coastline on the Gulf of Thailand in the southwest. The country is divided for administrative purposes into 20 provinces and three municipalities. The capital, Phnom Penh, is located in the southeast.

Two major water features, the Tonlé Sap (Great Lake) and the Mekong river dominate Cambodia's landscape. The Tonlé Sap is a vast lake in the country's central north-west, surrounded by a fertile plain. The Sap river runs from the lake's southeastern end to join the Mekong in Phnom Penh, some 100km (63 miles) away. During the dry months, roughly between November and May, the lake is at its smallest, though it still covers 2,500 to 3,000sq km (965 to 1,160sq miles). When the rains fall, though, from mid-May to October, a unique hydrographic phenomenon occurs. The rising waters of the Mekong cause the flow of the Sap river to reverse. During this period, the Tonlé Sap increases in surface area, sometimes to well in excess of 10,000sq km (3,860sq miles). At its lowest most of the lake is less than 2m (6.5ft) deep, and can resemble a marsh criss-crossed by navigable channels, but when at its fullest, its depth increases to as much as 14m (45ft), and it gains up to 70km (44 miles) in width.

Fishing village on Tonlé Sap

The Mekong enters from Laos close to Stung Treng in the north. It flows in a generally southerly direction for around 500km (312 miles), up to 5km (3 miles) wide in places, before crossing the border into Vietnam bound for the South China Sea. The river splits in two at Phnom Penh, the first major division of its large delta, which dominates southern Vietnam. The broader northern branch retains the name Mekong, while the southern branch is known as the Bassac.

Baguettes by the Mekong

Beyond the Mekong-Tonlé Sap Basin, Cambodia is fringed first by transitional plains, most of which are less than 100m (325ft) in elevation, and then by several mountain ranges on the peripheries of the country. The northern border with Thailand is marked by the Dongrak Mountains, a 350-km (220-mile) range of south-facing sheer sandstone cliffs rising 180 to 550m (600 to 1,800ft) above the Cambodian plain. In the southwest, covering much of the region between the Tonlé Sap and the Gulf of Thailand, two separate ranges, the Kravanh (Cardamom Mountains) and the Damrei (Elephant Mountains), form a remote upland area. It is here that Cambodia's highest peak, Mount Aoral at 1,813m (5,892ft), is found. Beyond these ranges, on the coast, is a narrow lowland strip, cut off from the central plains, and sparsely populated.

In the northeast of the country, occupying the remote provinces of Ratanakiri and Mondulkiri, the eastern highlands rise from the transitional plains. This region of thickly forested hills and isolated plateaus stretches east across the border into Vietnam, and north into Laos.

Khmer kids

Climate

Cambodia's climate revolves around the annual monsoon cycle. Between May and October, the southwest monsoon carries heavy daily rainfall, usually falling in the afternoons. The northwest monsoon, between November and March, brings slightly lower temperatures, and less precipitation. In between the monsoons are transitional periods, with changeable cloud cover, rainfall and high temperatures. The coolest months are between November and January, though even then temperatures rarely fall below 20°C (68°F). The driest months are January and February, when often there is no rainfall, and the wettest usually September and October. Rainfall varies considerably from region to region. The southwestern highlands, with their seaward-facing slopes, can exceed 5,000mm (200 inches) a year, while the central plains generally average 1,400mm (455 inches). Failure of the southwest monsoon can result in severe food shortages for the many Cambodians dependent on the Tonlé Sap and its surrounding fertile soils for their sustenance.

A large choice of greens

Population

Ethnic **Khmers** make up more than 90 percent of Cambodia's estimated 11 million people. The Khmers are a predominantly agricultural people, subsisting on a diet of rice and fish and living in wooden stilted houses in villages of several hundred people. Farming has long been the main occupation of the Khmers. Other traditional trades include weaving, pottery making and metalworking. In recent decades, as elsewhere in the developing world, there has been a marked degree of urbanisation as Khmers move to cities such as Phnom Penh, Battambang, Sihanoukville and Kompông Cham. The Khmers remain the dominant political and cultural section of the Cambodian population, though their economic influence

Signs of prosperity

7

Fish from Siem Reap

Muslim grave marker

Cham archers at Angkor

is far less on a per capita basis than that of the ethnic Chinese and Vietnamese.

The largest national minority within Cambodian society is the migrant **Vietnamese**. Because little love has traditionally been lost between Khmer and Viet, there is a tendency on the part of the Cambodian authorities to underestimate the number of Vietnamese in the country. Independent estimates put the figure at between 500,000 and 1 million. Cambodia's Viets tend to live either in the big cities, where they work as restaurateurs, tailors and in other small businesses, or along the Mekong and Sap rivers, where they fish.

A second distinctive minority in Cambodian society, which stands out chiefly because of its adherence to Islam, is the **Cham** Muslim. Originally migrants from the former Kingdom of Champa in what is today central Vietnam, the Chams were conquered by the Viets in the 17th and 18th centuries, resulting in the flight of many to neighbouring Cambodia. Today they live in scattered rural communities along the banks of the Sap and Mekong rivers, especially to the north of Phnom Penh. Gifted silversmiths, they also make a living by fishing and by butchering animals for their more fastidious Buddhist neighbours. There are thought to be between 400,000 and 500,000 Chams in Cambodia, despite having been particularly targeted for extermination by the Khmer Rouge.

Cambodia's ethnic **Chinese** are almost exclusively urban. Since they intermarry readily with the urban Khmers and are not disliked and feared like the Vietnamese, Chinese ethnicity is more readily subsumed within Khmer society. Most of Cambodia's Hua Chiao (Overseas Chinese), trace their origins to the southern coastal provinces of Hainan, Kwangtung and Fukien. Estimates as to their number vary from 100,000 to 400,000.

Other minorities include the **Khmer Loeu** (Upland Khmer) – autochthonous hill tribes of Mondulkiri and Ratanakiri, such as the Kuy, Mnong, Brao and Jarai, as well as the Pear and Saoch of the southwest. Strangely, several of these groups fared comparatively well under the murderous Khmer Rouge – usually ruthless in their treatment of national minorities – because they were seen as 'pure', unpolluted by capitalism and urban environment, and even as models of primitive communism. Collectively they probably number no more than 80,000.

Three groups who fared less well under the Khmer Rouge are the **Thai**, **Lao** and **Shan**. Faced with vicious discrimination between 1976 and 1979, those Thai who were not killed fled en masse to neighbouring Thailand. Similarly the Lao. The Shans – a few thousand resided in Pailin, where they worked as gem miners – were less fortunate, and seem to have been wiped out entirely.

Religion

Most Cambodians – around 90 percent of the population – are Buddhists. As in neighbouring Thailand and Laos, as well as in Burma and Sri Lanka, they are followers of the Theravada school (the 'Way of the Elders'). In contrast, the Buddhism practised in neighbouring Vietnam is Mahayana, as in China, Korea and Japan, a distinction which reinforces already deep cultural and social differences between the Khmer and Viet peoples.

Buddhism gradually spread throughout Cambodia from the 10th century on, receiving a boost during the reign of the Buddhist monarch Jayavarman VII (1181–1215). In time it replaced Hinduism as the state religion.

Theravada Buddhism emphasises personal salvation rather than the way of the *bodhisattva* associated with Mahayana teachings – that is, the temporary renunciation of personal salvation in order to help humanity to achieve enlightenment. The goal of the Theravadin is to become an *arhat* or 'worthy one'. This is considered to be one who has travelled the Noble Eightfold Path and, having eliminated the '10 fetters' or erroneous mental conceptions, attains Nirvana, or 'extinction'. In essence this means an end to corporeal existence and to the endless cycle of rebirth. Not many people seriously aspire to become *arhat* or achieve extinction in this life, that is usually seen as many lifetimes away. Instead, most Cambodians – like Thais, Lao or Burmese – aim for a better rebirth. This can be achieved by accruing good karma and minimising bad karma. In short, by being and doing good. Simple and effective ways of succeeding in this are considered to be by abstaining from taking life, refraining from alcohol, gambling and sexual promiscuity, keeping calm and not getting angry, honouring elderly people and so on. A very popular way of achieving merit is to give donations to temples and monks, whether this is represented by the expensive regilding of a stupa or the simple donation of a handful of rice to an itinerant monk.

Above all, honour and respect should be paid to the *triratana*, the 'Three Jewels' of Buddha, *sangha* (order of monks) and *dhamma* (sacred teachings). In consequence, nearly all Cambodian Buddhist men will join the *sangha* and become monks at least once in their lives. Women, too, may become ordained as nuns, though the percentage is lower and the decision is often delayed until middle or old age after having raised children.

Islam

Islam, perhaps surprisingly, is Cambodia's second religion. Nearly all Cambodia's Muslims are ethnic Chams, at around 500,000 people the country's second largest minority after the Vietnamese. Originally refugees from

Buddha at Udong

Monks with a view

Making offerings at a shrine

Sign for a new mosque

The Cresent Moon

18th-century Vietnam, the Chams practise a fairly lax form of Sunni Islam, fasting a day a week during the month of Ramadan, abstaining from pork but often drinking alcohol. Since the years of the Khmer Rouge, when Islam as a religion suffered particularly severely, aid in the form of money, new mosques, books and education from Malaysia and the Middle East is slowly resulting in the establishment of a more orthodox Sunni Muslim tradition.

Christianity
Christianity, introduced to Indochina by the French, never made much headway among the Buddhist Khmers. The Vietnamese, by contrast, were much more open to new religions, and several million became Catholic. Because of this, Christianity in Cambodia is more associated with expatriate Vietnamese – than with Khmers. This is probably why the Khmer Rouge went to the trouble of completely destroying Phnom Penh Cathedral. Today Christian missionaries are once again openly propagating the Bible.

Vietnamese religions
At upwards of one million people, the ethnic Vietnamese constitute the largest ethnic minority in Cambodia. Made up of a wide cross section of Viet society, they include representatives of all Vietnamese religious persuasions, including – besides Mahayana Buddhists, Confucianists and Christians – such exclusively Vietnamese faiths as Cao Dai and Hoa Hao Buddhism. The Holy See of the Cao Dai is located in the Vietnamese province of Tay Ninh, close to the Cambodian frontier, and this extraordinary syncretic religion – which counts Victor Hugo, Laozi and Jesus among its saints – has in some cases crossed the wide Viet-Khmer ethnic divide to win Khmer converts.

Painting spirit houses

Animism

Animism in Cambodia is generally limited to upland minority peoples (Khmer Loeu) such as the Kuy, Mnong, Brao and Jarai of northeastern Mondulkiri and Ratanakiri, and the Pear and Saoch of the southwestern Cardamom and Elephant Mountains. As in neighbouring Thailand, the spirit world is also very real to Cambodian Buddhists. Spirit houses are a frequent sight in Khmer homes, and tutelary spirits of good, bad and indifferent character are widely believed in and revered or respected.

Spirit house detail

Facing the world head on

11

Language

Khmer, also called Cambodian, is a Mon-Khmer language spoken by the majority of the people of Cambodia, as well as in parts of northeastern Thailand and southern Vietnam. It belongs to the Austro-Asiatic group of languages, which is widely spread throughout mainland Southeast Asia. Mon-Khmer languages, which are generally considered to have been some of the earliest established in the region, include Mon and Wa. Cambodian is a non-tonal language that has borrowed heavily from Sanskrit, Pali, Thai, Chinese and Vietnamese. It has been written since at least the 7th century, using a script derived from India.

Because of the difficulty of learning Cambodian script, visitors to the country are unlikely to achieve any great fluency in Khmer – though the lack of tones makes it easier for Westerners than, say, Vietnamese or Thai. It is relatively easy to acquire some basic vocabulary, however, and any such effort will be greatly appreciated by the locals. English is rapidly becoming the second language, especially in the cities of Phnom Penh, Siem Reap and Sihanoukville. Older people, particularly among the elite, may speak French.

Some members of the Sino-Cambodian community speak Guoyu, or Mandarin Chinese. Thai is widely understood in Battambang and the west of the country; similarly Vietnamese is widely understood in the east. Cham, the language of Cambodia's Muslim minority, is an Austronesian language related to Malay – but virtually all Cambodia's Chams are also fluent in Khmer.

English tuition notices

The monarchy

Samdech Preah Norodom Sihanouk, King of Cambodia, was born in Phnom Penh in 1922, the most recent in a long line of Cambodian monarchs stretching back to the *devaraja* 'God-Kings' of Angkor. He succeeded to the throne in 1941 and ruled as king until 1955, when he abdicated but retained power variously as prime minister, head of state and president. Ousted by the military coup of General Lon Nol in 1970, Sihanouk moved to Beijing and allied himself with the communist Khmer Rouge.

Portrait of King Sihanouk, Phnom Penh

The national flag

Victims of genocide at Tuol Sleng Museum, Phnom Penh

After the Khmer Rouge seizure of power in 1975, he returned to Phnom Penh only to be put under house arrest by his erstwhile 'allies'. Following the Vietnamese expulsion of the Khmer Rouge in 1979, Sihanouk became president-in-exile of the anti-Vietnamese coalition forces, spending his time in Beijing or Pyongyang. In September 1993, following UN-sponsored elections in Cambodia, he returned to Phnom Penh and resumed his position as king. His son, Prince Norodom Ranariddh, became 'First Prime Minister' and remains heir apparent.

The Khmer Rouge years must have been a difficult time for Sihanouk. Held under house arrest for three years, he watched powerlessly as at least a dozen members of his family were murdered by his KR jailers. The succeeding years must also have been hard, as he found himself in a variety of alliances with the still-powerful Khmer Rouge guerillas opposing the Vietnamese-backed regime in Phnom Penh. Certainly, when he returned to the throne in 1993 he seemed a somewhat chastened figure, weakened by illness and spending much of his time in Beijing.

But Sihanouk still retains widespread affection and loyalty among his people, many of whom would like to see the Cambodian monarchy emulate that of neighbouring Thailand, providing an anchor for national pride and constitutional stability. For the present, however, this seems unlikely, as Prince Ranariddh, King Sihanouk's likely successor, remains directly involved in Cambodia's complex political arena.

Politics and administration

In May 1993, following the United Nations-organised elections, Cambodia officially became a constitutional monarchy with King Norodom Sihanouk as Head of State. The Khmer Rouge opted out of the elections, however, and this led to more years of intermittent warfare during which the Khmer Rouge was gradually worn down. The Khmer Rouge leader, Pol Pot, died in 1998, while the last Khmer Rouge diehard, military leader Ta Mok, was captured near Anlong Veng in the north of Cambodia and taken for trial to Phnom Penh in early 1999. As a consequence the power of the once greatly feared Khmer Rouge seems to have been broken for ever. Meanwhile, the fate of three leading former Khmer Rouge officials – Nuon Chea, Khieu Samphan and Ieng Sary, who remain at liberty in the western town of Pailin – remains to be decided.

On the 'constitutional' front, following the 1993 elections Norodom Ranariddh became 'First Prime Minister', while the head of the former Vietnamese-backed regime, Hun Sen, became 'Second Prime Minister' in an unusual, and ultimately unworkable power-sharing arrangement. In July 1997 Hun Sen moved against Ranariddh through a short, swift coup d'état in Phnom Penh which forced the First Prime Minister to take refuge in France. Hun Sen emerged as the strongman of Cambodian politics, a position he has been gradually consolidating despite efforts by the opposition to destabilise his government. Although Cambodia's long-anticipated admission to the Association of South East Asian Nations (ASEAN) was initially postponed, the country became a member of this powerful economic alliance in April 1999. Elections were held once again in July of 2003. While Hun Sen won a majority of votes, his party failed to get the two-thirds majority prescribed by law. Opposition leaders Prince Ranariddh and Sam Rainsy refused to form a coalition, and at time of writing the stalemate had yet to be broken.

Cambodia-Vietnam Monument

Economy

The Cambodian economy has been virtually destroyed twice in recent decades. First when the Khmer Rouge entered Phnom Penh in 1975; and again with the 1989 withdrawal of the Vietnamese and the collapse of the Soviet Union, a major source of aid. Today, with Phnom Penh's move away from communist ideology to market economics, things are starting to improve a little.

Lasting damage

13

By far the greatest sources of foreign revenue are wood exports and foreign aid, neither of which is sustainable. A third significant revenue, also of dubious long-term soundness, derives from the shipment of gold and cigarettes from other Asian countries to Vietnam, where tariffs are significantly higher. Other than timber and gemstones, which are also a source of income, Cambodia has few natural resources. Rubber used to be a major export, with the Soviet Union purchasing almost the entire annual production, but it is now less important.

Just as in neighbouring Laos, heavy investment is needed in education, basic infrastructure and telecommunications before Cambodia will start to look attractive to major foreign investors. At the moment, both the government and outsiders seem mainly interested in fast profits, and few are looking at longer term, positive development. It can only be hoped that a more responsible view and approach will emerge before too much more damage is done.

Plying the Mekong

Inevitably, the economic possibilities of the Mekong river have not gone unnoticed in Cambodia. As in other countries on the Mekong, various proposals have been made, mainly revolving around the establishment of hydroelectric facilities. So far nothing has come of these proposals, but they have brought to light the serious risks posed to Cambodia by similar projects up-stream in Laos and China. Because Cambodia is so dependent on the annual rise in the waters of the Mekong and Tonlé Sap and

Temple musicians at Tonlé Bati

the fertile deposits this brings, any change in the flow of the river could potentially have disastrous effects on agriculture. The possibility of a decline in numbers and species of fish in the lake and river is also worrying.

For the foreseeable future, tourism may well be the greatest chance for Cambodia to secure clean, sustainable foreign exchange. After being completely wiped out under the Khmer Rouge, the tourist industry is growing stronger by the year, though current annual numbers of tourist arrivals remain considerably lower than they were back in the 1960s. But Angkor still stands, and remains one of the world's most marketable architectural and historical sites.

As the clearing of land mines continues, and facilities for tourist accommodation and transport gradually improve, there is little reason why this valuable resource should not be developed responsibly and successfully.

Nature and environment

Cambodia's central lowland plains are largely agricultural, but outside the cultivated fields of rice, maize and tobacco, they are thinly forested, with scrub-like areas of reeds and grasses covering large areas. Around the periphery of this area, the transitional plains are covered with savanna grasses and small bushes.

'Save our trees'

The various mountain ranges in the country support several different forest types. Large areas of the Cardamom and Elephant Mountains in the southwest are covered in virgin rainforest, where the upper canopy often reaches 50m (160ft). Elsewhere in these mountains, at the highest elevations, are sub-tropical pine forests. The eastern mountain ranges bordering Vietnam and Laos are covered with deciduous forests and thick grasslands.

Over the past three decades, large-scale logging has continued unabated throughout much of Cambodia. Estimates put the reduction in forest cover at around one-third since 1970. While the Khmer Rouge started the exploitation of the forests, post-Khmer Rouge governments have helped to accelerate it. With international demand for timber, and stricter controls on logging and the export of wood continually being imposed in surrounding countries, Cambodia has not hesitated in cashing in on its forests. Logging concessions have been sold to foreign nations, particularly Malaysia and Indonesia, bringing much-needed cash to the ailing economy, but with little, if any, thought of the future.

Rural idyll near Siem Reap

Another habitat at risk is the salt marshes and mangroves that make up the narrow strip of land on the coast between the southwestern mountains and the Gulf of Thailand. This delicate ecology is threatened by commercial shrimp farming, largely the province of Thai entrepreneurs. The method of raising prized tiger-shrimps in ponds is extremely destructive: mangroves must be cleared and farms become useless within about four years.

In the mid-1990s the first of 23 protected areas proposed by King Norodom Sihanouk was established in the south-western province of Kompong Speu. Most of the areas have now been set up, and when completed will afford official protection to around 15 percent of Cambodia's land. The various levels of protection include national parks, scenic zones, wild-animal sanctuaries, and so-called multi-use zones, in which some commercial activity will be permitted. The zoned regions are mainly located in the mountainous periphery of the country, though a few, including the Tonlé Sap area, are in the central plains.

Frangipani in blossom

Wildlife

Losses of forest cover and infringement on previously un-inhabited forests, together with many years of war, pose a serious threat to the country's fauna. Among Cambodia's larger animals are tigers, leopards, rhinoceroses, elephants, and various species of bear, deer and wild cattle. Many of these are threatened, along with a great many smaller mammals, including monkeys, squirrels, voles and rats. The country is also rich in bird life, and notable species include those found in wetland and grassland ecosystems such as cranes, herons, pelicans, cormorants, ducks, grouse and pheasants.

15

Out fishing at Tonlé Sap

Animal conservation still remains a minor issue in Cambodia. Many people still hunt – though thankfully the country is no longer, as it once was, a major game-hunting destination – and there is little education regarding the importance of maintaining a balanced ecosystem. Still, large sections of the country are still virtually uninhabited, and little visited by locals or foreigners, so there remains a chance that some areas will be preserved.

Farm life near Sihanoukville

Historical Highlights

4200BC Evidence of cave dwellers who fired pots found in northwestern Cambodia, though no corroborative links with present-day Khmers have been found.

1500–1000BC Ancient bones indicate physical similarity between these remote ancestors and today's majority Khmer population. Archaeological evidence indicates that these early Cambodians lived in stilt houses and consumed a protein-rich diet of fish, cultivated rice and salt.

100–600AD Establishment of a flourishing trading state called Funan in the Chinese Annals. Based on the fertile flat lands around Phnom Penh and Tonlé Sap, it seems to have served as a port for passing Indian, Arab and Chinese shipping. Funan also acts as a channel by which Indian religious traditions – initially Shiva and Vishnu worship, but subsequently Buddhism – enter the area. Ruins of Oc-Eo near Long Xuyen in southern Vietnam are generally associated with Funan's capital.

500–700AD A proto-Khmer state is established further inland from Funan, based near the confluence of the Mekong and Sap rivers. Known to the Chinese as Chen La, the inhabitants speak a Mon-Khmer language, worship Shiva and begin to create a distinctive Khmer form of art at Angkor Borei. The first great Khmer buildings are produced during the reign of Insavarman I (616–65) at Sambor Prei Kuk, the capital city northeast of the Tonlé Sap.

802–50 Reign of Jayavarman II, who proclaims himself a God-King and begins the enormous task of moving the capital to the Roluos region at Angkor.

877–89 Indravarman I creates a united Khmer Empire and begins the construction of a massive irrigation system that will underpin the future expansion of the state.

889–908 Yasovarman moves the capital from Roluos to Angkor, which he expands.

1113–50 Surayavarman again adds to the monuments, completing Angkor Wat and conquering part of the Cham lands to the east.

1181–1215 Jayavarman VII, perhaps the greatest of all the Khmer kings, builds the Bayon – thereby establishing the rising influence of Buddhism in the region – and Angkor Thom. He also subjugates the Chams, who had sacked Angkor in 1177.

1296 The Siamese, a growing power to the north and the west, capture and pillage Angkor.

1297–8 Chou Ta-kuan, a Chinese visitor to Cambodia, leaves the only contemporaneous written account of life and society in the Kingdom of Angkor.

1352–1430 The increasingly powerful Siamese Kingdom of Ayutthaya besieges, sacks and pillages Angkor on four separate occasions, taking away the Khmer court regalia and a great many prisoners.

1432 Under continuing pressure from the Siamese, the Khmer King Ponhea Yat determines to abandon Angkor, moving the capital southwards and eastwards to the Phnom Penh region near the confluence of the Mekong, Sap and Bassac rivers. Subsequently Lovek, to the north of Phnom Penh, becomes capital.

1593–4 Lovek captured by Thai King Naresuan.

1618–1866 Chey Chettha II moves capital to Udong on a large hill about 40 km (25 miles) north of Phnom Penh.

1859 The French land at Saigon and in 1862 they assume control over three provinces of Cochin China.

1863 French Admiral de la Grondière travels to Udong and forces King Norodom to sign a treaty making Cambodia a French protectorate. King Norodom effectively becomes a puppet ruler under the French.

1866 Capital established at Phnom Penh. King Norodom dies in 1904 and is succeeded by King Sisowath who rules until 1927 and is in turn succeeded by King Monivong. Finally, when Monivong dies in 1942 his successor, Norodom Sihanouk, becomes King of Cambodia.

1892 French troops seize the northwestern provinces of Cambodia from Siam and reincorporate them into the country. There follows a period of tension and some fighting between France and Siam, resulting in the imposition, by France, of the current Thai-Cambodia frontier in 1907.

1941 Taking advantage of World War II, Thailand invades and reoccupies northwestern Cambodia (Battambang and Siem Reap), only to be expelled in 1946 following the Japanese defeat.

1945 King Sihanouk declares Cambodian independence with Japanese support.

1953 Cambodia gains full independence from France under King Sihanouk; in 1955 Sihanouk abdicates, making his father, Suramarit, king, while retaining real powers himself.

1959 Cambodia breaks off diplomatic relations with Thailand over ownership of Preah Vihear. The case is sent to the International Court at The Hague which decides in favour of Cambodia.

1960s King Sihanouk becomes increasingly autocratic. Desirous of maintaining neutrality in the developing Vietnam War, Cambodia is caught between the demands of the North Vietnamese Army and Viet Cong on one side, and the United States and the forces of the Republic of Vietnam on the other.

1970 General Lon Nol deposes Sihanouk and establishes a US-backed Cambodian Republic. Many leftists – including senior Khmer Rouge leadership – flee to the jungle. Sihanouk retires to Beijing, where he supplies moral support for the Khmer Rouge. In an undeclared act of warfare, carpet bombing of central and eastern Cambodia begins by the United States.

1973 US troops begin to withdraw from Vietnam.

1975 Fall of Phnom Penh to Khmer Rouge, declaration of 'Year Zero' and the establishment of Democratic Kampuchea. Emptying of towns, establishment of a paranoid, rural-based Luddite regime with no ties to International Communism.

1976–8 The so-called 'Zero Years' are characterised by national chauvinism, religious intolerance, destruction of minorities, forced mass collectivisation and a frightening form of mass murder which has come to be described as autogenocide. This, combined with a rising wave of anti-Vietnamese militarism, leads to open conflict with Vietnam at several points along the southeastern frontier.

1979 Vietnamese invasion and occupation of Cambodia. Democratic Kampuchea leadership flees to the Thai border. There ensues a long period of guerilla warfare, with China, Thailand and most of the West backing the disgraced Democratic Kampuchea, while Vietnam and the Soviet Bloc together with India support the new government in Phnom Penh.

1979–88 Up to 100,000 Vietnamese forces are stationed in Cambodia at any one time to prevent a Democratic Kampuchea resurgence.

1989 Vietnamese forces start to withdraw.

1991 Prince Sihanouk returns to Phnom Penh.

1993 In May general elections are held under the supervision of the United Nations.

August 1998 The temple of Preah Vihear reopens to visitors. However, access remains limited to the Thai side.

1998 Pol Pot, the Khmer Rouge leader, dies. In April 1998, amid massive and continuing desertions, the Khmer Rouge lose their last stronghold at Anlong Veng to government troops. In late 1998 two surviving Khmer Rouge leaders, Nuon Chea and Khieu Samphan, arrive at the former Khmer Rouge stronghold of Pailin. Together with Ieng Sary, erstwhile Khmer Rouge leader and now strongman at Pailin, they are promised amnesty in a bid to promote 'national unity'.

1998–9 Hun Sen emerges as Cambodia's new strongman (*see page 13*), having cut a deal with the remaining Khmer Rouge leadership which leaves them powerless and isolated. He has politically emasculated Prince Norodom Ranarridh, King Sihanouk's heir, and left the remainder of the opposition divided and weak.

2002 The first multi-party local elections are held, won by the People's Party.

2003 Hun Sen's People's Party wins the general election but without a clear majority.

Wat Phnom

Preceding pages: Angkor Wat

Entrance to Wat Phnom

Buddha figures in the temple

Route 1

Phnom Penh

See map on page 22

Although it is possible to fly directly from Bangkok to Siem Reap, the airport for Angkor, for most visitors the gateway to Cambodia will be the capital, Phnom Penh. This will be even more the case when Pochentong International Airport is upgraded to receive long-haul flights from Europe and elsewhere. In fact, this isn't a problem. The Cambodian capital is an attractive riverside city of broad boulevards with numerous sights to please the visitor. It's still rather shabby and run down from the long years of war, not to mention four years of Khmer Rouge abandonment, but improvements are well under way.

City tour 1: the riverside

All of the more important attractions are located beside or within walking distance of the Phnom Penh riverside, an area which also has many of the best restaurants and cafés in town.

★ **Wat Phnom ❶**, built on a small mound in the north of the city not far from the banks of the Sap river, is an appropriate place to begin a tour of the waterfront. It is perhaps the most important temple in the capital, and from it the city takes its name. According to legend, around six centuries ago a Cambodian woman called Penh found some Buddha figures washed up by the bank of the Sap river. Being both rich and pious, she had a temple constructed to house them on top of a nearby hill – in fact a mound just 27m (88ft) high, but for all that the highest natural point in the vicinity – hence 'Phnom Penh' or 'the Hill of Penh'.

Wat Phnom, the temple built to house the figures, is entered from the east via a short stairway with *naga* balustrades. The main *vihara*, or temple sanctuary, has been rebuilt several times, most recently in 1926. There are some interesting murals from the *Reamker* – the Khmer version of the Indian *Ramayana* – and in a small pavilion to the south is a statue of Ms Penh, the temple's founder. Wat Phnom is eclectic to say the least. Although dedicated to Theravada Buddhism, it also houses (to the north of the *vihara*) a shrine to Preah Chau, who is especially revered by the Vietnamese community, while on the table in front are representations of Confucius and two Chinese sages. To the left of the central altar – lest anyone feel left out – is an eight-armed statue of the Hindu deity Vishnu. The large stupa to the west of the *vihara* contains the ashes of King Ponhea Yat (1405–67). Those who wish may make a short elephant ride around the mound on which the temple sits; there are numerous cold drinks vendors in the vicinity.

To the north of Wat Phnom, along 47th Street (also known as Vithei France), lie many dilapidated colonial buildings, increasing numbers of which are being renovated. This is the old **French Quarter ❷**. Should you wish to explore it, walk north along 47th Street to the roundabout, turn south down Monivong Boulevard past the French Embassy (on the right) and the British Embassy (on the left), before turning east by the railway station along 106th Street. If, on the other hand, this diversion seems too strenuous an addition to the tour, leave Wat Phnom by the main eastern stairway and walk due east to the Sap river, noting en route the colonial-style post office building, usually resplendent with large portraits of King Sihanouk and Queen Monique.

At the river turn right (south) along Sisowath Quay. This is a delightful area of small riverside cafés and restaurants where it is possible to savour the French influence in Cambodia's past – a good place, indeed, to stop for a breakfast of coffee and croissants, or a baguette with pâté. Alternatively, if the time for lunch is approaching, the **Foreign Correspondents Club of Cambodia ❸** is open to all comers, has a good bookshop on the first floor, and offers unsurpassed views across the Sap and Mekong rivers from its well-appointed second-floor restaurant.

Just behind the FCCC stands the imposing bulk of **Wat Ounalom ❹**, the headquarters of the Cambodian *sangha*, or Buddhist order. Founded in 1443, this extensive temple suffered badly at the hands of the iconoclastic Khmer Rouge, but is fast recovering. Unfortunately the once

Mural at Wat Phnom

Waiting elephant

Foreign Correspondents Club

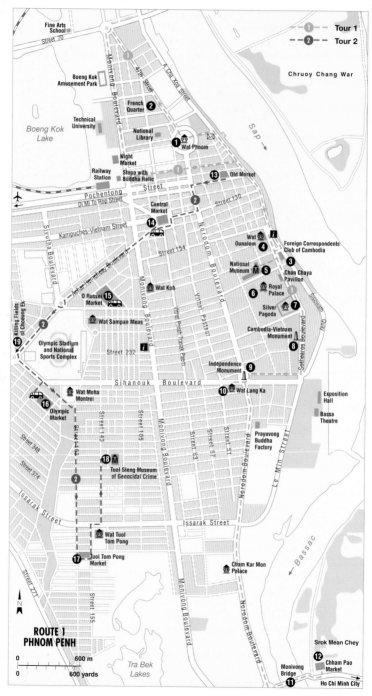

ROUTE 1
PHNOM PENH

extensive library of the Buddhist Institute, which is also housed here, will take many years to replace. To the west of the main temple stands a stupa said to contain an eye-brow hair of the Buddha. Within the temple are several archaic Buddha figures, which were smashed to pieces by the Khmer Rouge but have since been reassembled. Also on display is a statue of Samdech Huot Tat, head of the Cambodian *sangha* when Pol Pot came to power and sub-sequently killed by the Khmer Rouge; it was recovered from the nearby Mekong and reinstalled after the collapse of Democratic Kampuchea.

Continuing southwards, the visitor will soon come to a small (and rather unkempt) public garden which lies in front of the ★★ **National Museum** ❺ (Tuesday to Sunday 8am–noon and 2–5pm; closed Monday). The museum, housed in a red pavilion built in 1918, holds a wonder-ful collection of Khmer art, including some of the finest pieces in existence. It also once 'housed' an estimated two million bats in its attic. Recently the bats were removed after it was determined that their acidic droppings were damaging the museum's priceless works. It's a good idea to purchase a copy of the museum guidebook, *Khmer Art in Stone*, at the entrance desk. This identifies and discusses the most important exhibits, including a 6th-century statue of Vishnu, a 9th-century statue of Shiva, and the famous sculpted head of Jayavarman VII in meditative pose. Particularly impressive is a damaged bust of a reclining Vishnu which was once part of a massive bronze statue found at the Western Mebon Temple in Angkor.

National Museum

Immediately south of the museum lie the extensive grounds of the ★★ **Royal Palace** ❻ (daily 7.30–11.30am and 2.30–5pm), built in Khmer style with French assis-tance in 1866. The palace functions as the official residence of King Norodom Sihanouk since his return to the capital in 1992 – though the king still spends much of his time in Beijing, which seems to have become his second home. The entrance for visitors is opposite the attractive, colonial-style Renakse Hotel, to the east of the palace grounds. Certain areas within the palace, including the king's residential quarters, are off-limits to the general public, but much of the complex is accessible. A sign at the gate – doubtless soon to be removed as security improves – informs the visitor that guns and explosives are not to be taken inside.

Just beyond the entrance gate stands the **Chan Chaya Pavilion**, formerly used by Cambodian monarchs to review parades and for performances of classical Khmer dancing. Nowadays performances of the latter are regu-larly given at the nearby Hotel Cambodiana – those in-terested in witnessing this beautiful spectacle should check

Royal Palace exterior and door panel of the Royal Throne Hall

Chan Chaya Pavilion

with the Cambodian Tourist Board (*see page 88*) or at the Cambodiana reception desk (*see page 93*).

Dominating the centre of the larger northern section of the royal compound is the **Royal Throne Hall**. This was built as recently as 1917, the architect self-consciously borrowing extensively from the Bayon style at Angkor. Inside, the walls are painted with murals from the *Reamker*, the Khmer version of the *Ramayana*. Apart from coronations, the Throne Hall is used for important constitutional events and, on occasion, for the acceptance of ambassadorial credentials.

Napoleon III Pavilion

To the right (northwest) of the Throne Hall stands the restricted **Royal Residence Compound** of King Sihanouk, while to the left (south) are several structures of interest, including the **Royal Treasury**, the **Royal Banqueting Hall** and the **Napoleon III Pavilion**. This latter building, which has recently been renovated by French volunteers, was originally given by the Emperor Napoleon III to his wife the Empress Eugenie, who in turn had it dismantled and sent to Phnom Penh as a gift for King Norodom in the 1870s.

Leaving the main northern compound by a clearly marked gateway in the southeastern corner, the visitor should then proceed along a narrow southwesterly route to the North Gate of the celebrated ★ **Silver Pagoda** ❼ compound. This structure, so named because its floor is lined with more than 5,000 silver tiles weighing more than 1kg (2lb) each, or 5 tonnes in total, is also known as **Wat Preah Keo**, or 'Temple of the Emerald Buddha'. Like its famous namesake in Bangkok, it is considered to house the palladium of the nation, and – again, as in Bangkok – photography within the building is forbidden. The Silver Pagoda was built by King Norodom in 1892, and extensively rebuilt by King Sihanouk in 1962. It houses two priceless Buddha figures, one of which – the Emerald Buddha, from which the temple gets its name – dates from the 17th century and is made of crystal. The other is a much larger affair, being made of 90kg (1.8cwt) of pure gold, encrusted with 9,584 diamonds, the largest of which is 25 carats.

Silver Pagoda and mural detail

Leaving the palace and proceeding south along Sothearos Boulevard, the visitor will pass an extensive park on the right (west). In the centre of this park stands a statue in heroic Socialist-Realist style depicting two soldiers – one Vietnamese, the other Cambodian – protecting a Cambodian woman and child. This is the **Cambodia-Vietnam Monument** ❽, dedicated to the supposedly unbreakable friendship that links the two peoples. Unfortunately not all Cambodians agree with this sentiment, and the monument has been attacked and even set on fire with petrol

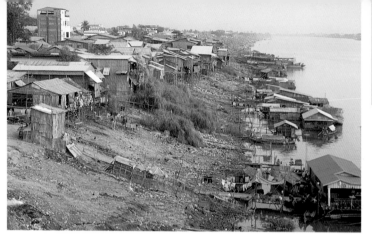

Along the banks of the Bassac

at times of political tension. Signs of damage are clearly visible to the head of one of the soldiers, though no one seems to be really sure which soldier is Vietnamese and which Cambodian.

By continuing to the southern end of the park and turning west along Sihanouk Boulevard, the visitor will reach the pineapple-shaped **Independence Monument** ❾. In fact, the monument represents a lotus and was built to celebrate Cambodia's independence from France in 1953. Located immediately to the south of this monolith is **Wat Lang Ka** ❿, the second Phnom Penh temple (after Wat Ounalom) to have been restored after the overthrow of the Khmer Rouge regime. Today the temple is a flourishing example of the revival of Buddhism in Cambodia. Saffron-robed monks abound, while newly painted murals from the *jataka* (Buddha life cycles) fairly gleam from the restored *vihara* walls.

Wat Lang Ka

While this riverside tour thus far offers wonderful views over the junction of the Sap and Mekong rivers, to really understand the unusual confluence of waters at Phnom Penh the visitor should also see the Bassac river. This is best viewed from the **Monivong Bridge** ⓫ south of the city centre, marking the start of Highway 1 leading to Ho Chi Minh City.

Monivong Bridge

The confluence of the four rivers, known in Khmer as ★ *Chatomuk* (four faces), and in French as *Quatres Bras* (four arms), is remarkable for a unique phenomenon, the reversal of the Sap river. From May to October, during the annual rainy season, the hugely increased volume of the Mekong forces the Sap river to back up, and finally reverse its course, flowing northwards to flood Tonlé Sap with vast quantities of fresh water and rich sediment. During this period Tonlé Sap more than doubles in size, from 3,000sq km (1,160sq miles) to as much as 10,000sq km

Chham Pao produce

(3,860 sq miles). Then, in mid-October, as the level of the Mekong diminishes, the flow of the Sap is again reversed, carrying the surplus waters of Tonlé Sap southwards to the Mekong and Bassac deltas. The time of the October reversal of the waters is celebrated as *Bon Om Tuk*, one of Cambodia's most important festivals. The annual flooding of Tonlé Sap makes the lake an amazingly rich source of fish, while the farmland around the lakes benefits from an annual deluge of rich sediment.

The detour to the Monivong Bridge can be combined with a visit to bustling **Chham Pao Market ⑫**, on the east side of the bridge in Srok Mean Chey district.

City tour 2: markets and memorials

Although the main attractions of Phnom Penh are congregated along the riverfront, there are several other interesting and worthwhile places to visit in the city, notably the main markets, including the most unusual Art Deco Central Market and the antique stalls and souvenir booths of Tuol Tom Pong Market. The last two destinations on this tour are horrific, but essential viewing for those with an interest in Cambodia's recent history, for to visit Tuol Sleng and Choeung Ek is a sobering reminder of the 'Zero Years' of the Khmer Rouge and Democratic Kampuchea (1975–9).

Vendors at the Old Market

While Chham Pao Market may be visited in conjunction with viewing the Bassac (*see above*), Phnom Penh has many more accessible markets for the visitor to see. Interestingly, the Khmer word for market, *psar*, is thought to be derived from the Arabic word *bazaar*, a reminder of the long presence of Arab and Indian traders in Southeast Asian waters. Most Cambodians still do their everyday shopping at the marketplace – though an increasing number of western-style supermarkets is appearing around town – and a visit to several of Phnom Penh's markets is always a worthwhile experience. A point to remember is that bargaining is expected. One might try making a starting offer at least 50 percent lower than the initial asking price – the locals won't be offended, and you can always walk away to try your luck elsewhere.

Perhaps the longest-established market in Phnom Penh is the *psar char*, or **Old Market ⑬**, located near the riverfront at the junction of 108th and 13th Streets. It's a densely packed locale offering a wide selection of tapes, books, clothing, jewellery, dry goods and fresh vegetables. Unlike some of the markets, it stays open late into the evening.

A short distance to the southwest, at the commercial heart of the capital, is the extraordinary *psar thmay*, literally 'new market', but generally known in English as ★ **Central Market** . It was built in 1937 during the French colonial period in Art Deco style and is painted bright ochre. The design is cruciform, with four wings dominated by a central dome, and the overall effect has been likened to a Babylonian ziggurat. In and around the four wings, almost everything is for sale including electronic equipment, tapes, videos, stationery, clothing, timepieces of all sorts, bags and suitcases and a wide variety of dried and fresh foodstuffs. Beneath the central dome are many gold and silver shops selling skilfully crafted jewellery, as well as Khmer *kramaa* (scarves), antiques, pseudo-antiques and other souvenir items.

O Russei Market

Proceeding southwest along Achar Hemcheay Boulevard, the visitor comes to **O Russei Market** ⑮, which sprawls between 182nd and 166th Streets. Nearly everyone in the market is local, and the goods on display reflect their demand for fruit and vegetables, flowers, fresh meat, bicycle and motorbike parts, new and second-hand clothing, etc. The market is inter-linked with a busy bus station, so watch out for reversing vehicles.

Olympic Market browsers

Continuing down Achar Hemcheay, also known as Charles De Gaulle (many of Phnom Penh's streets and boulevards have two or even three names, reflecting the political loyalties of changing regimes over the decades), the visitor should turn east on Sihanouk Boulevard and approach the **Olympic Market** ⑯, via 199th Street. This is another bus station-cum-bazaar, but rather more up-market than O Russei. It stocks a wide variety of products, including luxury goods such as imported perfumes and liquor, as well as clothing and jewellery and canned *pâté de fois gras*.

Finally, and perhaps most interesting for the visitor after the Central Market, ★ **Tuol Tom Pong Market** ⑰ (also known as the Russian Market) is situated in the

Treasures of Tuol Tom Pong

southern part of town, beyond Issarak Boulevard (also known as Mao Tse-tung Boulevard) at the junction of 163rd and 432nd Streets. This is probably the best place in town to shop for genuine and imitation antiquities, Buddha figures, silk clothing, silver jewellery, silver ornaments, gems and old bank notes from previous regimes. Interestingly, the bank notes for sale include those of the infamous Khmer Rouge, which had currency printed in China but then changed its mind, outlawed money and markets, blew up the central bank and ultimately never issued any notes to the public. Khmer Rouge money is readily recognised both by its pristine condition – it was never circulated – and by the warlike themes apparent on the notes. Look for rocket-toting guerrillas, howitzers, machine guns and fierce-faced Khmer Rouge girl soldiers.

Conditions at Tuol Sleng

28

Which brings us to the last, least likely and most disturbing part of this tour. Not for the weak-hearted, just over 1km (½ mile) from Tuol Tom Pong, to the north of Mao Tse-tung Boulevard, stands the former Tuol Sleng Prison, now ★ **Tuol Sleng Museum of Genocidal Crime** ⓲ (daily 7–11.30am and 2–5.30pm). Here, during Pol Pot's years in power, around 20,000 people were interrogated under torture and subsequently murdered, generally together with their families. The former prison – once a school – is a chilling sight. The pictures of many of those killed stare out at the visitor in black and white from the museum walls. The primitive instruments of torture and execution are on display, as is a bust of Pol Pot. Many of the former classrooms were divided up in an incredibly primitive fashion into tiny breeze-block cells. Everywhere there are crude shackles and cuffs. Initially, those executed here were people the Khmer Rouge perceived as 'class enemies' and supporters of the former regime, but soon the communist regime began to consume itself in a frenzy of paranoia. By the time Tuol Sleng was liberated in 1979, nearly all those suffering torture and execution were Khmer Rouge officials who had fallen from grace.

A country of skulls

Among the Killing Fields

For those with the stomach for the experience after visiting Tuol Sleng, about 12km (7½ miles) south of town lie the infamous **Killing Fields of Choeung Ek** ⓳. Here victims of the Khmer Rouge, including many from Tuol Sleng, were taken for execution and burial in mass graves. Many of these have now been exhumed, and a stupa-shaped mausoleum has been erected to their memory. It's a disturbing experience to view row upon row of skulls, arranged in tiers in a tall Plexiglass case in the middle of the mausoleum. The easiest way to get there is by taxi from the vicinity of the Central Market, though motos waiting outside Tuol Sleng will also make the journey.

Route 2

Shrine at Udong

North of Phnom Penh

**Chruoy Changvar – Cham Villages – Udong – Lovek
– Kompông Cham – Wat Nokor Bayon – Mekong River**
See map on page 30

29

Udong, a former royal capital of Cambodia, can be visited
with ease from Phnom Penh on a day trip. Should you have
the time and the inclination, a more rewarding and infor-
mative trip can be made by continuing by road to stay
overnight in the large Mekong port city of Kompông
Cham, returning by boat to Phnom Penh the next day. In
this way a small circular tour can be made encompass-
ing royal tombs, rubber plantations, an important Hindu
temple and a voyage down the great Mekong river.

The former royal capital of Udong is located on low hills
about 35km (22 miles) north of Phnom Penh. The road
to Udong is Highway 5, which continues to Kompông
Chhnang, an important river port on the Sap river 60km
(38 miles) north of Udong. Highway 5 winds north out
of Phnom Penh on the west bank of the Sap river. As you
drive north you will notice the **Chruoy Changvar Peninsula** between the Sap and Mekong rivers to the east. If you
look closely, you will see small minarets indicating the
presence of two or three mosques in the rural villages of
the peninsula. The name 'Changvar' is said to be derived
from the island of Java in Indonesia, and the peninsula
is home to one of Cambodia's fascinating but sadly
decimated Cham Muslim communities – a people who
suffered hideously under the Khmer Rouge regime.

Scenes on the Sap river

Chruoy Changvar is reached by the 'Japanese Bridge'
(in 1993 it was rebuilt with Japanese aid) and makes an

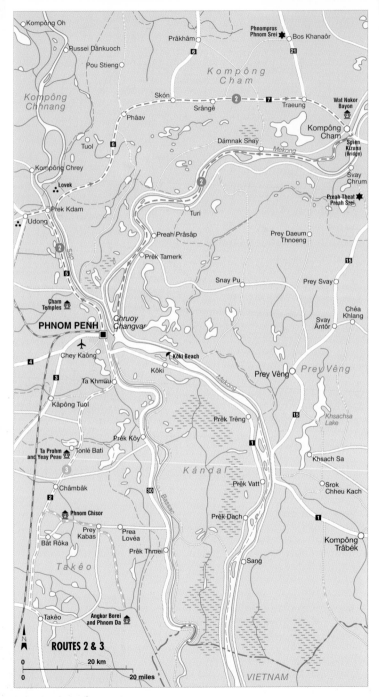

30

Kompóng Oh

Russei Dănkuoch

Pou Stieng

Prăkhâm

Phnompros
Phnom Srei
Bos Khanaôr

*Kompóng
Cham*

6

21

*Kompóng
Chhnang*

Skón

Srăngĕ

2

7

Traeung

Wat Nokor
Bayon

Phăav

Tuol

6

Dămnak Snăy

Mekong

Kompóng
Cham

Spien
Kizuna
(Bridge)

Kompóng Chrey

Lovek

Turi

Svay
Chrum

Preah Theat
Preah Srei

Prĕk Kdam

2

Udong

Preah Prăsăp

Prey Daeum
Thnoeng

Prĕk Tamerk

Snay Pu

Prey Svay

15

2

5

Cham
Temples

*Chruoy
Changvar*

Svay
Ântôr

Chéa
Khlang

PHNOM PENH

Koki Beach

Prey Vêng

4

Chey Kaóng

Kóki

Mekong

Prey Vêng

3

Ta Khmau

Kăpóng Tuol

Prĕk Trêng

15

*Khsachsa
Lake*

Prĕk Kôy

1

Ta Prohm
and Yeay Peau

Tonlé Bati

3

Kándal

Khsach Sa

Chămbâk

30

Bassac

Prĕk Vatt

Srok
Chheu Kach

2

Phnom Chisor

Prea
Lovéa

Prĕk Dach

1

Bât Rôka

Prey
Kabas

Prĕk Thmei

Kompóng
Trâbék

Takêo

Sang

Takêo

Angkor Borei
and Phnom Da

N

ROUTES 2 & 3

0 ——— 20 km

0 ——— 20 miles

VIETNAM

interesting extra two-hour trip from Phnom Penh, being particularly popular with city residents for its fine riverside restaurants. For Udong, however, ignore the bridge and continue north, passing through several prosperous **Cham villages** with newly restored mosques and silversmiths' workshops. The locals are friendly, and it's all right to visit the mosques and photograph the turbaned Cham men, though – as with Buddhist temples – shoes should be removed before entering a place of worship.

★ **Udong** – the name means 'victorious' – was the capital of Cambodia on several occasions between 1618 and 1866. Today little remains of the former capital's days of glory, but the site is still worth a visit. Two small hills rise from the surrounding plains. Unfortunately, both bear the marks of extensive bombing during the war years, and many of the stupas have been destroyed or are in ruins. The larger of the two hills is called Phnom Reach Throap, or 'Hill of the Royal Treasury'. Here one can see the remains of an enormous Buddha figure – blown up by the Khmer Rouge – as well as stupas containing the ashes of King Monivong (ruled 1927–41), King Norodom (ruled 1845–59) and the 17th-century ruler King Soriyopor.

Udong detail

31

A short distance northeast of Udong, but not easily accessible by road, is another former royal city called **Lovek**. Situated on the west bank of the Sap river, Lovek was an interim Cambodian capital between the times of Angkor and Udong which flourished in the 16th century. In 1594 Lovek was captured and looted by the burgeoning Kingdom of Ayutthaya (Siam). According to legend, the Siamese besieged the city in 1593, but were beaten back. Before leaving, however, they used cannon to fire silver shot into the bamboo fortifications surrounding Lovek. After their withdrawal, the Cambodians tore down these barricades to get at the silver. As a consequence, when the Siamese returned a year later, they took the city with ease. This legend may well not be true, but it is closely associated with the years of Cambodian decay that followed the abandonment of Angkor, and looking at Lovek today – or what can be seen from the banks of the Sap river – the former city seems symbolic of that period of decay.

Downtown Lovek

After visiting Udong backtrack down Highway 5 for 4km (2½ miles) to the small town of **Prek Kdam** on the banks of the Sap river. From here it's a short ferry ride to the east bank of the river, then a 42-km (26-mile) drive along Highway 6 to the junction town of Skón. The countryside is fertile and verdant (especially during the rainy season), with rice paddies and clusters of sugar palms stretching in every direction. From Skón follow Highway 7 for

Ferry at Prek Kdam

47km (30 miles) to Kompông Cham through countryside increasingly rich in rubber plantations.

Kompông Cham is Cambodia's third-largest city and an important communications hub. There are no major attractions in the city itself, though there are some interesting old colonial buildings, and the Mekong Hotel, located right on the waterfront, provides a pleasant location to have a drink or something to eat while watching life on the great river.

Colonial style in Kompông Cham

Riverside stalls

Just outside the town – about 2km (1 mile) to the northwest – there *is* a major attraction, however. ★ **Wat Nokor Bayon** is an 11th-century sandstone and laterite temple, originally dedicated to Mahayana Buddhism. At some time, probably during the 15th century, it was rededicated to Theravada Buddhism, and a modern temple set amid the ancient ruins still functions as a Buddhist centre today. The whole complex is a fascinating blend of the contemporary and the archaic. There are numerous niches containing Buddha images, and one large reclining Buddha. Wat Nokor Bayon is a good place to visit at sunset.

Wat Nokor Bayon and niche detail

After staying overnight in Kompông Cham, the traveller should board an express boat to Phnom Penh the next morning. The service is fast and fairly frequent – it takes about two hours to reach the capital. The journey can be quite fascinating. Small boats with one or two fishermen cast their nets and drift slowly downstream. Numerous ferryboats ply the river, and quite large cargo ships chug upstream against the muddy waters, ready to take on or offload cargo. Much of Cambodia's considerable rubber exports leave the country on these, sailing through Vietnam to the South China Sea. It's a novel way of seeing the countryside, and an increasingly comfortable way of travelling on one of the world's great waterways.

Route 3

South of Phnom Penh

Tonlé Bati – Ta Prohm – Yeay Peau – Phnom Chisor – Takêo – Angkor Borei – Phnom Da *See map on page 30*

Takêo Province, due south of Phnom Penh and bordering Vietnam, is a worthwhile destination offering the visitor a chance to see some fine examples of Khmer temple architecture. Because it is so close to Phnom Penh it is possible to visit some of these temples on a day trip from the capital. An interesting alternative is to stay overnight in the provincial capital – called Takêo, like the province – backtracking to visit the temples at leisure. Highway 2 from Phnom Penh to Takêo is a good road, and the journey should take only 1 to 1½ hours. Takêo is a quiet country town that makes a pleasant enough place to stop for the night. The hotels are adequate, and both Khmer and Chinese food is available. One would scarcely guess that during the Khmer Rouge period Takêo was the headquarters of Ta Mok, the much-feared one-legged general now imprisoned in Phnom Penh. 'Grandfather Mok' and his cadre made Takêo just about the most feared zone in the country, though there is little sign of those days now.

It is advised that the traveller takes two days over this route, setting out from Phnom Penh early in the morning and heading directly to ★ **Tonlé Bati** which is about 32km (20 miles) away. The chief attraction at Tonlé Bati is the laterite temple of **Ta Prohm** built by King Jayavarman VII on top of an earlier 6th-century Khmer shrine. The result is a well-preserved gem of a temple, not unduly large, but with some splendid decorative features. The main sanctuary has five chambers, in each of which is a statue or a Shiva *lingam*. At times the shrine is favoured by fortune-tellers who will predict your future and read your palm for a few riel. If you're lucky, one or two monks may be playing traditional musical instruments.

One unusual feature of the temple may be found on the east wall of the sanctuary, about 3.5m (11ft) above the ground. This is a bas-relief showing a woman carrying a box on her head while a man bows in supplication to another, larger woman. The story represented is that of a pregnant woman who gave birth with the help of a midwife, but then failed to show sufficient respect to the latter. As a punishment, the midwife has condemned her to carry the afterbirth in a box on her head for the rest of her life. The man is begging the midwife to forgive his wife. Another bas-relief on the inner north wall of the central sanctuary shows a king sitting with his wife. Because

Ta Prohm at Tonlé Bati

Lotus sellers at the temple

A story in stone

the latter has been unfaithful, a servant is represented in the lower part of the carving putting her to death by trampling her with a horse.

A further 150m (488ft) north of Ta Prohm is the second of Tonlé Bati's attractions, the much smaller temple of **Yeay Peau**. According to legend, during the early 12th century King Preah Ket Mealea fell in love with a young girl called Peau. Soon she became pregnant, and after a while gave birth to a boy whom she named Prohm. The king, meanwhile, had returned to Angkor, leaving a ring and a sacred dagger so that the boy could travel to Angkor and identify himself to his father when he came of age. In time this came to pass, and Prohm visited Angkor where he lived with his father for several years. On his return to Tonlé Bati, Prohm failed to recognise his mother, seeing instead a woman so beautiful that he asked her to become his wife. Peau objected that she was Prohm's mother, but the young man refused to believe this. Accordingly, it was decided that a contest should be held to see what should happen. If Prohm, assisted by the local men, could build a temple before Peau, assisted by the local women, could do so, then she would marry him. In the event the wily Peau created an artificial morning star using candles. The men, thinking it was dawn and that the women could not possibly beat them, went to sleep. The women went on to win the contest, and Prohm was obliged to acknowledge Peau as his mother. Inside the temple there is a statue of Peau beside a seated Buddha.

Yeay Peau

After seeing the sights at Tonlé Bati, the traveller should continue south on Highway 2 for around 23km (14 miles). The intersection for ★ **Phnom Chisor** is indicated by the two brick towers of Prasat Neang Khmau (Temple of the Black Virgin), once possibly dedicated to Kali. There is a left-hand (eastwards) turning at this point leading to the foot of Phnom Chisor about 4km (2½ miles) further on. It's about a 100m (325ft) climb to the top of the hill, but it's worth the effort because of the spectacular views over the surrounding countryside.

The main temple at Phnom Chisor stands on the eastern side of the hill. Constructed of brick and laterite with lintels and doorways of sandstone, the complex dates from the 11th century when it was known as Suryagiri. The isolation of the site, and the way the temple suddenly appears as the visitor struggles up the 500-odd steps, has led some writers to liken the temple's atmosphere to that of a Southeast Asian Stonehenge or Macchu Pichu.

Phnom Chisor

Fallen lintel

Having visited Phnom Chisor, it is best to press on to **Takêo**. There won't be a lot happening there, though – one should eat, have a few quiet drinks, and retire early with a view to an equally early morning start. As is the case

elsewhere in Cambodia, some of the very best light for photography is in the two hours after sunrise – or, indeed, the two hours before sunset.

Some light refreshment

35

In the morning head back northwards along Highway 2 until you reach the turning east to Phnom Chisor. Follow this road beyond the hilltop temple, through the town of **Sai Waa**, until you reach **Prey Kabas**. Just before the settlement, a side road leads to the southwest and, about 5km (3 miles) away, the busy little market town of **Angkor Borei**. It is believed that 12 centuries ago Angkor Borei was the site of Vyadhapura, capital of 'Water Chen La' before the centre of Khmer civilisation moved to Angkor. Unfortunately, there is little evidence of this to be seen. The area has yet to be thoroughly excavated, though American archaeologists from the University of Hawaii have been collaborating with their local counterparts in a preliminary survey. The visitor should check out Angkor Borei District Office, a pleasant old colonial-style building, where some Chen La artefacts are displayed, including temple carvings, early inscriptions and a Shiva *lingam*.

Children at Angkor Borei

The temple of ★ **Phnom Da** can be reached by crossing the bridge to the south of Angkor Borei and driving for 5km (3 miles). The hilltop temple, which may date from the 7th or 8th centuries, is of brick and sandstone. Although one of the oldest stone structures in Cambodia, it is in a surprisingly good state of preservation. Nearby on another hilly outcrop is a smaller sandstone temple, thought to have been built about a century after Phnom Da, called **Asram Taa Asey**. This structure is believed to have been dedicated to Harihara, a god combining manifestations of Vishnu and Shiva.

A word of caution about the Phnom Da region: during the rains the area floods and it is necessary to travel in a small boat from Angkor Borei.

The coast at Kâmpôt

Route 4

The Coast

Kâmpôt – Bokor – Kep – Kirirom – Sihanoukville (Kompông Som) – Koh Kong *See map on page 37*

Ochental Beach, Sihanoukville

While there can be no question that the major tourist destinations in Cambodia are Phnom Penh and, above all, Angkor, other regions are gradually opening up to visitors. Some such destinations – for example Ratanakiri and Mondulkiri in the northeast – are completely new attractions. The Cambodian coast, once hailed as the 'Cambodian Riviera', has long had a reputation as an idyllic tourist spot. Between about 1968 and the mid-1990s, however, all that came to an abrupt and vicious end, but now trips to the coast and long hours of swimming or sunbathing beneath swaying coconut palms are well and truly on the way back in.

There are two roads south from Phnom Penh to the coast. The dilapidated Highway 3 via Angk Tasaom to Kâmpôt; or the much better Highway 4 via Kompông Speu, to Sihanoukville (also known as Kompông Som) – considered by many the best road in the country. The 150-km (94-mile) drive from Phnom Penh to Kâmpôt takes about two hours by taxi or three hours by bus. The train, though functioning, cannot yet be recommended.

Kâmpôt, the capital of the province of the same name, is a small, laid-back town of around 15,000 people. Located just 5km (3 miles) inland, by the banks of a small river, the place has a coastal feel which adds to its rather bucolic attraction. There isn't a lot to do in town itself, but there are some pleasant examples of colonial architecture and an interesting market filled with vegetable produce (Kâmpôt province, incidentally, is the durian (fruit) capital of Cambodia). Still, Kâmpôt is a good place to use as a base for exploring the surrounding countryside, with adequate hotels and good provincial food available. Because it remains almost completely free from the pressures of tourism, the local people – friendly throughout Cambodia – seem especially charming.

Kâmpôt shelters in the lee of the Damrei (Elephant) Mountains, a wild region of trackless forests and sheer, unclimbed rock outcrops. Just two hours northwest of Kâmpôt, along a dubious road, is the former hill station of **Bokor**. Renowned in pre-war days for its pleasant climate, cool mountain streams, forested walks and distant panoramic view of the Gulf of Thailand, Bokor fell on hard times under the Khmer Rouge and has not yet really recovered. Still, it's worth a trip if you're in the vicinity. The 1,079m (3,506ft)-high resort is often shrouded in mist which drifts through the ruined casino and blown-up church. Soon, no doubt, it will be rehabilitated and once again echo to the sound of day-trippers from nearby Sihanoukville (Kompông Som).

Another formerly celebrated resort is **Kep**, known to the French as Kep-sur-Mer. In pre-war times the 7-km (4-mile) stretch of palm-fringed beach was lined with the

Downtown Kâmpôt

Pier at Kep

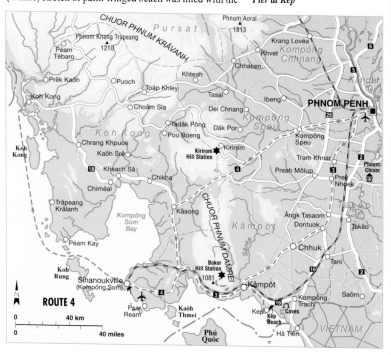

Destroyed villa in Kep

Sihanoukville railway station sign

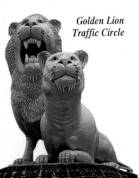

Sihanoukville snacks

Golden Lion Traffic Circle

villas of rich Cambodians and French settlers. Then the Khmer Rouge arrived and took a special vengeance on the place, destroying virtually every building in town and turning the Shell petrol station into the site of a mass grave. Today Kep is back on the tourist circuit, though much rebuilding remains to be done. It's a 30-km (19-mile) drive from Kâmpôt and can be reached by moto. Although there are hotels and restaurants – indeed, these are multiplying at quite a rate – most visitors will prefer to stay in Kâmpôt, driving out to Kep for a day of sunbathing, fishing, swimming and indulging in the excellent local seafood. Like Bokor, it won't be long before Kep is once again firmly back on the tourist map.

It is possible to travel from Kâmpôt to Sihanoukville directly, using the poor road alongside the equally run-down railway line, but most people will prefer to use Highway 4 from Phnom Penh to Sihanoukville. This is 230km (144 miles) long and requires two to three hours to cover by bus or taxi.

The road to Sihanoukville passes through the small provincial town of Kompông Speu before rising over a forested spur of the Damrei Mountains. Just before the small settlement of Sre Khlong a dusty road rises into the mountains leading to the former hill station of **Kirirom**. Once the hot-season retreat of wealthy Phnom Penh residents, it was – like Kep – deliberately blown up, building by building, by the vengeful Khmer Rouge. At present Kirirom is still less developed than Bokor, but as the centre of Cambodia's first officially designated national park it should in time flourish once again.

After crossing the Damrei Mountains, Highway 4 forks as it drops down to the coast. The eastern fork leads to the fishing port of Psar Ream, while the western fork continues to ★ **Sihanoukville** (Kompông Som).

For the present – indeed for the forseeable future – Sihanoukville will remain the heart of Cambodia's 'Riviera'. Like Kep, this town was once a haven for the rich, but the Khmer Rouge wrought less thorough destruction here, doubtless because Sihanoukville's deep-water port and railway terminus provide key international access to Phnom Penh. Nowadays the resort is packed on weekends with visitors from Phnom Penh. There are numerous hotels and guesthouses of all classes, many run by expatriate westerners. Sihanoukville's restaurants offer a wide choice of cuisine, the seafood is fresh and plentiful, and the traffic remains relatively light. The main activities are sunbathing and swimming. There's some good snorkelling, and diving trips are available with experienced divers. In all, Sihanoukville has about 10km (6 miles) of beachfront, divided into four main beaches.

Starting in the north, these are **Victory Beach** (between the harbour and Koh Pos Island); **Independence Beach** (between the old Independence Hotel and the southwestern peninsula); **Sokha Beach** (between the peninsula and the Cambodian army base); and **Ochental Beach**, stretching away south of the town. Of the beaches, Ochental is probably the most attractive, though all offer the craning palm trees and clear blue waters one would expect.

Ochental Beach

The coast to the west of Sihanoukville is almost completely undeveloped. There are no roads hugging the coastline around Kompông Som Bay, and a journey overland to the isolated but beautiful province of Koh Kong requires a long detour inland by Highway 48, which recently underwent an upgrade. However it only takes a monsoon or two before roads deteriorate. At time of writing the trip by road took between five and seven hours. There is also a daily ferry in both directions. There are speedboats that can do the trip in three to four hours. During the rainy season trips are sometimes cancelled when seas are rough.

★ **Koh Kong** – confusingly the name of the province, provincial capital *and* offshore island – is a rapidly-developing coastal resort designed especially to appeal to visitors from neighbouring Thailand. It is also a convenient point for entering or leaving Cambodia by land. Hardly surprisingly, the place has something of a Thai feel to it. In fact, before the 'Zero Years' of the Khmer Rouge, Koh Kong was largely settled by Thais who had lived there for generations. After the KR victory, most fled across the nearby border to Thailand, though some remained to carry on a surprisingly successful resistance from the jungles of the interior. Those who fell into KR hands, like most minorities elsewhere in Cambodia, were simply killed.

39

Koh Kong

Today Koh Kong has something of a Wild West feel to it. It's just 10km (6 miles) by taxi from the border post of Ban Hat Lek, and the presence of Cambodia's larger neighbour is everywhere to be felt. Nearly all consumer goods on sale in town are trucked or ferried in from Thailand. A new casino has been built on Cambodian territory just opposite Ban Hat Lek, which attracts many Thais keen to enjoy the gambling denied them by law at home. Perhaps inevitably, numerous bars and brothels have also sprung up to cater for this rapidly expanding trade.

At the market

Should you decide to leave Cambodia via Koh Kong, fast air-conditioned buses depart from the city of Trat on the Thai side of the border on a regular basis. Depending on the traffic and the time of day, it takes around five hours to reach Bangkok's eastern bus terminal.

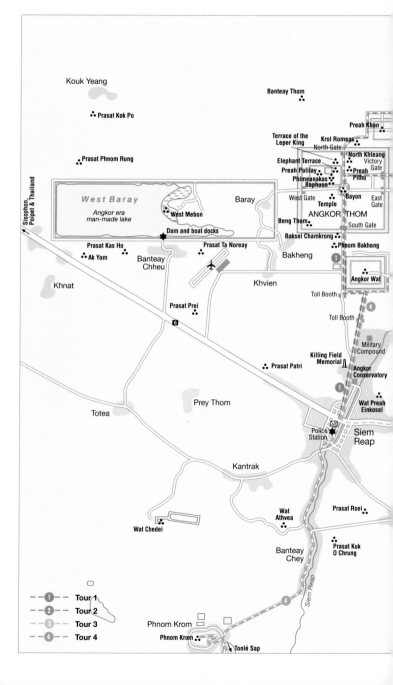

Kouk Yeang

• Prasat Kok Po

Banteay Thom

Preah Khan

Terrace of the
Leper King   Krol Romeas
North Gate

Prasat Phnom Rung

Elephant Terrace   North Khleang
Victory
Preah Palilay   Preah   Gate
Phimeanakas   Pithu
Baphuon

Sisophon,
Poipet & Thailand

West Baray
Angkor era
man-made lake   Baray

West Gate   Bayon   East
Temple   Gate

West Mebon   ANGKOR THOM

Dam and boat docks   Beng Thom   South Gate

Prasat Kas Ho   Prasat Ta Noreay   Baksei Chamkrong

Ak Yom   Banteay
Chheu   Bakheng   Phnom Bakheng

Khnat   1

Khvien   Angkor Wat

Prasat Prei   Toll Booth   4

6   Toll Booth

Military
Compound

Killing Field
Memorial   Angkor
Prasat Patri   Conservatory

1
Prey Thom   Wat Preah
Einkosel

Totea

Police   Siem
Station   Reap

Kantrak

Prasat Rsei

Wat
Athvea   Prasat Kuk
O Chrung

Wat Chedei   Banteay
Chey

1   Tour 1
2   Tour 2
3   Tour 3   Phnom Krom
4   Tour 4   Phnom Krom
Tonlé Sap

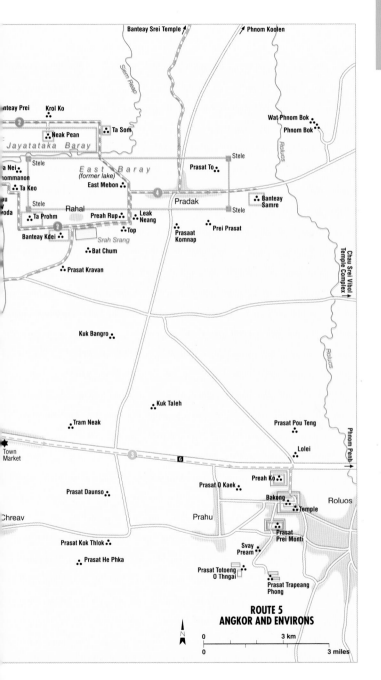

Banteay Srei Temple ↗

Phnom Koolen ↗

Siem Reap

Banteay Prei

Krol Ko

Wat Phnom Bok

Phnom Bok

Neak Pean

Ta Som

Jayatataka Baray

Stele

a Nei

E a s t   B a r a y
(former lake)

Prasat To

Stele

hommanon

Ta Keo

East Mebon

au

Stele

Rahal

Pradak

Banteay
Samre

oda

Ta Prohm

Preah Rup

Leak
Neang

Stele

Prei Prasat

Banteay Kdei

Top

Prasaat
Komnap

Srah Srang

Bat Chum

Chau Srei Vibol
Temple Complex

41

Prasat Kravan

Kuk Bangro

Riohuos

Kuk Taleh

Tram Neak

Prasat Pou Teng

Lolei

Phnom Penh

Town
Market

6

Preah Ko

Prasat Daunso

Prasat O Kaek

Bakong

Roluos

Temple

Chreav

Prahu

Prasat
Prei Monti

Prasat Kok Thlok

Svay
Pream

Prasat He Phka

Prasat Totoeng
O Thngai

Prasat Trapeang
Phong

**ROUTE 5
ANGKOR AND ENVIRONS**

↑
N

0   3 km

0   3 miles

Angkor Wat

Route 5

Angkor and environs

Although the visitor will surely have seen photographs and read descriptions of the temples before visiting them, nothing can truly prepare one for the immense scale that is the reality of Angkor. Perhaps nowhere else on earth, unless it be the Valley of the Nile in Egypt, are the relics of antiquity found on so monumental a scale.

Background

Angkor was the capital of the Khmer Empire from the 9th to 15th centuries. From here a dynasty of Khmer kings ruled one of the largest, most prosperous and most sophisticated kingdoms in the history of Southeast Asia, which in its heyday extended from the tip of the Indochinese peninsula northwards to Yunnan and from Vietnam westwards to the Bay of Bengal.

A blend of styles

During the period of construction at Angkor, which lasted more than 300 years, many changes in architecture and artistic styles can be discerned, and there was a religious movement from the Hindu cult of the god Shiva to that of Vishnu to a Mahayana Buddhist cult devoted to the *bodhisattva* Avalokitesvara. The city was finally abandoned in 1432, after the armies of the Thai kingdoms had begun to encroach on the Khmer heartland. Angkor Wat, the most famous temple at Angkor, was taken over by Theravada Buddhist monks and became an important pilgrimage site. The remainder of the 'lost city' had to wait until the arrival of the French colonial regime, when archaeologists began unravelling the mysteries of the past and embarked on a painstaking programme of reconstruction and restoration, which continues to this day.

Tour 1: the central temple complex

The road to Angkor leads north from Siem Reap, past a monument to the victims of the Khmer Rouge 'Killing Fields' and the Angkor Conservatory, to a tollbooth. Here the visitor must pay a fairly hefty charge – at the time of writing, US$20 per day, US$40 for three days, US$60 for four days to a week – before proceeding to view the monuments. About 1km (½ mile) beyond the tollbooth the road reaches the south side of Angkor Wat, and the visitor will catch first sight of the world-famous monument. For the moment, however, it is probably best to drive past Angkor Wat by the west road and visit the city of Angkor Thom, as the former is most impressive in the afternoon when the complex is best illuminated by the sun.

Children of Angkor

★★★ **Angkor Thom** ('Great City') encompasses a huge area of land within a square surrounded by an 8m (26ft)-high defensive wall and outer moats approximately 100m (325ft) wide. Each side of the wall is about 3km (1¾ miles) long, and it has been speculated that, at the height of its wealth and power, the city may have supported as many as one million people. The founder was King Jayavarman VII (1181–1215), probably the most prolific builder the Khmer Empire ever produced. Today the wooden and bamboo buildings that constituted the major part of the city have long since disappeared, but the great stone religious monuments are still in evidence.

Angkor Thom: the South Gate

There are five *gopura* gateways into the city, each approached by a causeway built across the moat. As the visitor approaches from the south, the initial impression of the fortifications of Angkor Thom is indeed impressive. The causeway is flanked by 108 large stone figures, 54 gods on the left and an equivalent number of demons on the right. Both gods and demons support a great *naga* snake on their knees. At the start of the causeway these *naga* raise their nine heads in a fan-shaped motif. In the distance, at the far end of the causeway, the southern *gopura* – one of the most mystic, and certainly one of the most photographed monuments at Angkor – bears four huge enigmatic faces facing in the cardinal directions.

Passing through this prodigious gateway, the road continues northwards for around 1.5km (1 mile) to reach a roundabout marking the centre of Angkor Thom. Here, in the very heart of the city, stands the justly celebrated ★★★ **Bayon**. This temple, which is best entered from the east, was built in the late 12th century by the Buddhist Jayavarman II, the architect of Angkor Thom. Always a favourite with visitors, the Bayon is possibly the most celebrated structure at Angkor after Angkor Wat itself.

Strangely, until the discovery of a Buddhist front in 1925 bearing a figure of Avalokitesvara, the Bayon was thought to be a Hindu temple dating from 900AD. It is now

The Bayon rises like a mountain

Pig fight in bas-relief

Khmer warriors

believed to post-date Angkor Wat by about a century, though the structure remains one of the most enigmatic and puzzling at Angkor. This may be because the Bayon, as it exists at present, was built on top of an earlier temple, which was almost certainly Hindu. The new aspects of the temple created by Jayavarman VII include 54 towers bearing more than 200 huge, serene stone faces. Some hold that these faces portray the *bodhisattva* Avalokitesvara, but most authorities accept that they represent the omnipresence of the man who ordered their construction, King Jayavarman VII.

The Bayon is thought to represent a symbolic temple mountain. Certainly, it rises on three levels, the first of which bears eight cruciform gateways. These were linked by galleries which were once covered and which may soon be so again – extensive restoration is currently under way. These galleries contain some of the most remarkable bas-reliefs at Angkor, and are well worth an hour or two of the visitor's time. They combine numerous domestic and everyday scenes with historical details of battles fought and victories won and lost by the Khmers. The domestic scenes, many of which are in smaller bas-reliefs below the main war scenes, show such things as fishermen, market scenes, festivals, cockfights, pig fights, giving birth, playing chess, removing lice, hunting with bows and arrows, and so on. There are also everyday scenes from the royal palace – princes and princesses, wrestlers, sword fighters, general scenes of entertainment.

To view the bas-reliefs it is best to start near the east entrance and proceed clockwise, via the south wall, keeping the bas-reliefs to your right. The **East Gallery**, which is in an excellent state of preservation, features a military procession of Cambodian troops, elephants, ox carts, horsemen and musicians. Parasols shield the commanders of the troops, who include King Jayavarman VII. The ★ **South Gallery** is spectacular and contains some of the finest bas-reliefs at Angkor. The early panels depict the great naval battle that took place at Tonlé Sap in 1177. The Khmers have no head coverings and short hair, while the Cham invaders wear strange hats that resemble long hair. The fighting is intense, with bodies falling from the boats sometimes being taken by crocodiles. Further along the gallery the Chams are shown disembarking and attacking, only to suffer defeat. Later Jayavarman VII is seen sitting in his palace while his Khmer subjects celebrate their victory. Proceeding along the western end of the Bayon, the visitor comes to the **North Gallery**. Here you should look for fine carvings of jugglers, acrobats, wrestlers and various animals, including pigs, rhinoceroses, rabbits, deer and lobsters. There are further scenes of combat between the Chams and the Khmers, with the Khmers apparently at one point fleeing to the hills. The **Interior Galleries** include more military scenes of Cham and Khmer warriors, battle elephants and details from everyday life. On the southern gallery Vishnu and Shiva make appearances, a tiger devours a man, and princesses walk amid groups of *apsara* dancing on lotus flowers.

Having viewed the galleries, the visitor should climb to the third level and spend some time examining the vast, mysterious faces with their sublime smiles. The central shrine, which is circular, is also at the third level and features the faces of the *bodhisattva* Avalokiteshvara.

Cham warrior

Leave the Bayon by the northern *gopura* and walk along the road towards the north gate of Angkor Thom. After about 500m (¼ mile) on the left (or western) side of the road you will reach the **Baphuon**. At present this is largely collapsed, but an extensive restoration programme is under way. The Ecole Français d'Extrème Orient was in the process of carrying out this restoration as long ago as 1972, but had to abandon the project when the war made such endeavours too risky.

The Baphuon

Baphuon is a temple mountain representing Mount Meru. Originally a central tower with four entrances stood on the peak, but it has long since collapsed. The Baphuon is approached by an elevated causeway 200m (650ft) long. At present access for visitors is restricted, but it is possible to walk to the western extremity where a carved reclining Buddha may just be seen spanning the length of the west platform. Since Baphuon was an early Hindu temple, built by Udayadityavarman II (1050–66), we may safely assume that this reclining Buddha figure was a later addition, dating perhaps from the 15th century.

Immediately to the right and north of Baphuon stands the badly decayed royal palace enclosure, again currently

More Bayon motifs

Phimeanakas

46

Elephant Terrace

undergoing restoration. The most important structure here is **Phimeanakas**, the 'aerial palace'. Built during the 10th and 11th centuries, it was the work of several kings, but was founded by King Rajendravarman II (941–68). Phimeanakas is a relatively small structure, but nevertheless significant as the temple where the king himself worshipped.

Dedicated to Hinduism, the temple is also associated with the legend of a golden tower (*phimeanakas*) inside the royal palace where a nine-headed serpent lived. The serpent appeared to the king as a woman, and the monarch would congress with this serpent-woman in the golden tower every night before joining his wives and concubines elsewhere in the palace. It was thought that if the king failed in this obligation he would die. In this the royal lineage of the Khmer kings was assured.

Although Phimeanakas is dilapidated, it is worth climbing to the upper terrace to obtain a fine view of the nearby Baphuon. Turning the other way, northward, two pools become visible. The smaller and deeper is called **Srah Srei**, the women's bathing place.

Directly in front of Baphuon and Phimeanakas, to the west of the road to the north gate, stand two terraces that merit careful examination. The first and largest of these is the ★ **Elephant Terrace**. Built by Jayavarman VII, this structure is over 300m (975ft) long, and stretches from the Baphuon to the nearby Terrace of the Leper King. It has three main platforms and two lesser ones. The terrace was probably used for the king, members of the royal family, ministers and generals to review their forces and, perhaps, to watch other entertainments. The whole terrace is elaborately decorated. There are the sandstone elephants from which the terrace gains its name, but also tigers, lions,

naga, garuda, sacred geese and lotus flowers all presented in a wealth of detail.

Immediately to the north of the Elephant Terrace and in a direct line with it stands the ★ **Terrace of the Leper King**. Like the Elephant Terrace, this much smaller structure dates from the late 12th century and is the work of Jayavarman VII. In fact, the identity of the so-called 'leper king' is surrounded by mystery and uncertainty. Nowadays it is generally accepted that this headless statue, which sits with its right knee raised on top of the terrace, represents Yama, the god of judgement and death. The original statue has long since been removed to the courtyard of the National Museum in Phnom Penh, and the statue on top of the terrace today is a replica. It is, nevertheless, impressive. It may be that the so-called 'Terrace of the Leper King' was once a royal crematorium.

Leper king statue and apsara

Statue aside, the terrace is remarkable for its many bas-reliefs. The structure, which is about 6m (20ft) high, is supported by a base 25m (81ft) on either side. Built of laterite faced with sandstone, the exterior wall is adorned with snakes, *garuda*, many-armed giants, *apsara*, soldiers, fish, elephants – indeed all manner of decorations. When members of the French Ecole Français d'Extrème Orient were restoring the terrace, they discovered a collapsed inner wall which has now been restored and is accessible via a narrow passageway built behind the exterior wall. This enables the visitor to inspect both walls in comfort.

47

Turning from the Terrace of the Leper King, the visitor should head southwards back to the Bayon and leave Angkor Thom via the south gate. A few hundred metres beyond the south gate, to the west side of the road, the hill of ★ **Phnom Bakheng** rises 67m (218ft) above the surrounding plains. This is an ideal spot to view the distant spires of Angkor Wat at sunset, but is well worth climbing at any time of the day. On the east side of the hill a steep and treacherous stairway provides a swift but difficult means of ascent. Alternatively, a winding elephant path leads to the summit via the south side of the hill. Its flat top bears a large temple, Bakheng, from which the hill derives its name. Built in the late 9th century by King Yasovarman I, this is a Hindu structure dedicated to the god Shiva.

Having descended Phnom Bakheng, the visitor should continue south for around 1.5km (1 mile) to the western entrance to ★★★ **Angkor Wat**. By any standards, this must be the highlight of any visit to the Angkor region – the great temple is simply unsurpassed by any other monument. Construction of this masterpiece is thought to have begun during the reign of Surayavarman II

Angkor Wat: the main causeway

(1113–50), and to have been completed some time after his death. Authorities claim that the amount of stone used in creating this massive edifice is about the same as that used in building the great pyramid of Cheops in Egypt, though at Angkor there are many more exposed surfaces, nearly all of which are elaborately carved.

Angkor Wat was established as a Hindu temple dedicated to the god Shiva, but it is also thought to have been envisaged as a mausoleum for Surayavarman II. Its orientation is different from most temples at Angkor, as the main entrance is from the west, rather than from the east. The bas-reliefs – one of the most important elements of the temple – are intended to be viewed from left to right, conforming to Hindu practice. The westward orientation of the temple is supposed to be related to the association between the setting sun and death.

The sheer scale of Angkor is difficult to grasp in a single visit. Just walking to the central shrine across the moat and along the main causeway is a humbling experience. At the end the main towers of the temple rise to an astonishing 65m (211ft) through three separate levels. At the third level there are five great towers – one at each corner, and the great central spire. These towers are conical in shape, tapering to a lotus-patterned point.

The moat

According to the great French archaeologist Georges Coèdes, Angkor Wat – literally translated, the name means 'the city which is a temple' – is a replica of the universe. The central tower represents Mount Meru, located at the centre of the universe. The outer walls symbolise the mountains at the edge of the world, and the surrounding moats the oceans beyond.

The area of land covered by the complex is around 210 hectares (500 acres), surrounded by a moat which is 200m (650ft) wide. Yet despite these overwhelming statistics, Angkor is a very human place. Vendors of all kinds of goods, from cold drinks and snacks to the ubiquitous sarongs, *kramaa* (Khmer scarves) and cast heads of Jayavarman VII and other kings, are everywhere. Cattle wander across the main temple enclosure and drink at the tanks there, while buffalo laze and flick their tails in the broad moats surrounding the complex. Take it easy exploring Angkor Wat and stay out of the sun. The site is so large and so worthwhile that two visits at least are certainly in order should one have time.

Refreshment at hand

The approach to the main temple sanctuary is along a raised path approximately 350m (1,138ft) long by 9m (30ft) wide. This causeway is flanked by *naga* balustrades on either side. Two buildings, loosely defined as 'libraries', stand on either side of the causeway about halfway to the main complex. Cruciform in shape, they are exquisitely

*Khmer generals
on horseback*

decorated and certainly merit a brief diversion from the path. To the east of the libraries are two reservoirs, only one of which is still lined with stone, which capture the reflection of the sanctuary towers during the rainy season.

Proceeding along the central causeway the visitor should enter the central sanctuary at the first level and turn right to circumambulate the entire gallery of bas-reliefs – no small feat, as there is much to see. Shortly after entering the first gallery you will pass a huge standing stone figure with eight arms bearing symbols which indicate that the statue was of Vishnu. In recent times, however, Vishnu's head has been replaced by a Buddha head, and the statue is now much venerated by local Buddhists.

The bas-reliefs of Angkor's first-level galleries are truly remarkable, but some stand out as being a cut above the rest. The visitor should look out for the following:

West Gallery
The Battle of Kurukshetra: The southern part of the west gallery depicts a scene from the great Hindu epic, the *Mahabharata*, in which the opposing Kauravas and Pandavas clash with each other. Foot soldiers are at the lowest level, with officers on elephant back, and in the upper tiers. Areas of the bas-relief have been touched and caressed by human hand over so many centuries that in places the sandstone looks like gleaming black marble.
The Battle of Lanka: This panel shows a well-known scene from the *Ramayana* and must be considered one of the finest bas-reliefs to be found at Angkor Wat. It depicts a long struggle between Rama and the demon-king of Lanka, Ravana. The battle culminates with the defeat of Ravana and the liberation of Rama's wife, Sita. This panel is particularly distinguished by the fine representations of Hanuman's monkey army, whose lithe figures are exceptionally finely carved.

Vishnu turned Buddha

Siamese mercenaries

South Gallery

The Army of King Surayavarman II: This splendid panel shows the victorious army of Surayavarman II in triumphal march. Surayavarman rides a great war elephant and carries a battle axe. He is shaded by 15 umbrellas and fanned by numerous servants. The main ranks of Khmer soldiery march in close order and look like serious warriors. To the west is one of the earliest representations of Thais, at this time fighting as mercenary troops for the Khmer Empire. In contrast to the serried ranks of the Khmers, the Thais can be seen marching out of step. They wear long dress-like sarongs and headdresses, and are carrying tridents.

Going to hell

The Scenes of Heaven and Hell: The scenes on this panel, depicting the various punishments and rewards of hell and heaven, are truly terrifying. Those who have done well and accumulated merit in this life seem to be fine. They approach Yama, the judge of the dead, together with his two assistants, Dharma and Sitragupta, apparently confident of passage to heaven. Beneath them, however, sinners are being dragged to hell by hideously powerful devils wielding heavy black clubs. Yoked in groups of four, the condemned suffer terrible tortures.

Churning of the Ocean of Milk

East Gallery

The Churning of the Ocean of Milk: This is probably the best-executed and most spectacular of all the bas-reliefs at Angkor. In one huge, brilliantly carved panel, 88 *asura* (devils) on the left (south side) and 92 *deva* (gods) on the right (north side) churn the sea of milk with a giant serpent for 1,000 years. Their purpose is to extract the elixir of immortality, which both covet. Overhead finely carved *apsara* sing and dance to encourage the gods and devils in their endeavour. By any standards, this is a truly remarkable work of art.

The Victory of Vishnu over the Demons: Vishnu, riding on a *garuda*, is engaged in mortal combat with legions of devils. Perhaps predictably, the powerful god takes on all comers and, despite the odds, emerges victorious.

• Note that the central gateway in the East Corridor has no steps, and it would be possible to fall some distance to the hard stone floor beneath. This is the 'elephant gate' used by kings to enter Angkor from the east. It is designed to be high enough for the monarch to walk directly off an elephant's back and on to the terrace.

North Gallery

The Victory of Krishna over Bana: In this panel Vishnu, in his incarnation as Krishna, rides a *garuda*. A burning walled city is the residence of Bana, the demon king. The *garuda* puts out the fire and captures Bana; then, in a spirit of mercy, Krishna kneels before Shiva and asks that the life of the demon king be spared.

The Battle between the Gods and the Demons: This finely carved panel features yet another battle scene. Here 21 gods of the Brahmanic pantheon struggle with various devils. The gods are distinguishable by their traditional mounts and aspects. Shiva, for example, rides a sacred goose, while Vishnu has four arms and is seated on a *garuda*.

Having examined the galleries of bas-reliefs, the visitor should enter the central complex and climb up to the second level by the usual steep flights of steps (this is no place for sufferers from vertigo). The exterior of this level is rather plain compared with what has gone before and what is to come, and it has been suggested that the simplicity was designed to provide an atmosphere suitable for calm and contemplation among the many priests who would once have concentrated here. Within the second level, however, there is a plethora of *apsara* – more than 1,500 celestial dancers – lining the walls and providing endless distraction to the visitor, as they must once have done to the priests and royal family.

The climb to the third level is steeper and more vertigo inducing than what has gone before. This level was recently put off limits to visitors after a tourist was seriously injured during a fall. It is unclear whether or not this is just a temporary measure, but should this level be open when you visit, keep in mind that it should probably be skipped if you have any doubts.

In times past, only the king and the high priest were allowed on the upper (third) gallery of Angkor Wat. The central sanctuary rises 42m (137ft) above the upper level, bringing the overall height of the central tower at Angkor to the same height as the cathedral of Notre Dame in Paris. There are four porches opening to the cardinal directions, all of which once gave access to a statue of Vishnu. Today, in the overwhelmingly Theravada Buddhist Kingdom of Cambodia (*see page 9*), Vishnu has given way to a modern image of the Buddha.

The central sanctuary and the third tier of Angkor are ideal places to visit at sunset. Stunning views are available across the entire temple, and – perhaps for the first time – it is possible clearly to grasp the stupendous size of the complex. As the sun goes down, warm, golden or red rays of sunshine pierce the elaborately carved sandstone window buttresses, illuminating the very finest and best-preserved *apsara* to be found anywhere at Angkor. Truly, it is an unforgettable experience. Because of the steepness of the narrow stairways, don't wait until it is dark before making your descent – night falls quickly in the tropics.

The main towers

Apsara at sunset

Tour 2: outer temples

The outer temples of Angkor comprise, by and large, the main sites once grouped together by the French as the 'Grand Circuit'. While the central complex can be explored by bicycle and even, at a pinch, on foot, the outer temples are so widely spread that a car or motorbike is essential. Despite the distances, a visit to the outer temples is highly recommended. From the cloistered wonder of Preah Khan, through the 'medicinal baths' of Neak Pean, to the jungle-covered glory of Ta Prohm, the outer temples are simply magnificent.

From Siem Reap head north past Angkor Wat, through Angkor Thom, to the north gate. It is possible to stop here and climb the wall to the left of the gateway – taking care not to slip on the exposed tree roots – and photograph the heads above the gateway in profile. Next, turning due east, stop opposite the row of cold drinks stalls directly in front of the west entrance to ★★★ **Preah Khan**, the temple of the 'sacred sword'. This magnificent structure was founded by King Jayavarman VII (1181–1215). Built in the style of the Bayon (*see page 43*) and dedicated to the Buddhist religion, the temple served as a monastery and teaching place, the centre of a former royal city located on the Jayatataka Baray (a former reservoir). Other temples associated with Preah Khan include nearby Neak Pean and, somewhat further to the east, Ta Som. It has been suggested that Preah Khan may have served as a temporary capital for Jayavarman VII at the time when he was rebuilding Angkor Thom following the sacking of that city by the Chams in 1177.

There is a magical quality about Preah Khan, not unlike that of Ta Prohm, which comes from the feeling of closeness to nature. In part this is because the temple still awaits

Preah Khan with mythical singha

full restoration, and great trees with smothering roots still cling to the sandstone and laterite walls. Not for much longer, however, as the temple is currently being restored, and many of the old trees have been felled. Beyond the walls of the temple, however, the jungle still reigns supreme, adding to the mystery and numinous quality of the location.

An inscribed stone stele, found at Preah Khan in 1939 and removed for safe-keeping to the Angkor Conservatory, indicates that the temple was once the heart of the ancient city of Nagarajayacri. The central sanctuary was dedicated in 1191, when the Buddhist Jayavarman VII ruled at Angkor. Jayavarman, however, was followed by a series of Hindu-oriented kings who did their best to Hinduise the great Buddhist sanctuary of Preah Khan. Accordingly, images of the Buddha were chipped out of their niches, and elsewhere in the interior of the shrines Buddha images were transformed into *rishi*, or ascetics, by the simple addition of beards.

Preah Khan's library building

53

Preah Khan is a huge complex. If it seems anything less than this, it is simply because of the proximity of the even larger city of Angkor Thom. The site covers around 57 hectares (140 acres). A laterite wall about 3km (2 miles) long surrounds the whole complex, with carved *garuda* guardian figures facing outwards every 45m (146ft). Access to the central sanctuary is by four massive cross-shaped *gopura* at the cardinal points of the compass. The best way to enter the temple is through the eastern gateway, though most taxi drivers will try to drop you at the west gate and collect you from the northern one. The approach ways to the various gates are spectacular – paved causeways are lined with gods (on the left) and demons (on the right) pulling the body of a serpent to churn the primordial ocean of milk in a 1,000-year search for the elixir of immortality.

The central sanctuary of Preah Khan is cruciform, with four entranceways. Look for the 'Hall of Dancers', named after the finely carved rows of *apsara* that decorate the walls. If you are feeling fit and agile enough to clamber over (and sometimes under) the great piles of fallen stone in the northeastern section of the main sanctuary, you may visit the 'Shrine of the White Lady'. Here an elegant figure, supposedly not an *apsara* but the wife of King Jayavarman VII, is tucked away in a hidden room. The shrine is still venerated, and supplicants light incense and leave offerings of money. You will need a guide to find this out-of-the-way spot, but the effort is worth it.

Shrine of the White Lady

After leaving Preah Khan, preferably by the north *gopura*, the visitor should head eastwards along the road leading to the East Baray. About 2.5km (1½ miles) from Preah

Neak Pean

Khan a track leads southwards for around 300m (1,000ft) to the highly unusual temple of ★★ **Neak Pean** ('Coiled Serpents'). This structure, which dates from the latter half of the 12th century, was built by the ever-active King Jayavarman VII and – as always, with this monarch – was dedicated to the Buddhist faith. Located in the midst of the Jayatataka Baray, Neak Pean now remains dry for most of the year, but it was once an island, and its whole purpose is closely connected with water.

The temple, which is quite small by Angkorean standards, is set in an artificial reservoir 70m (230ft) square. This central pool is surrounded, again at the cardinal points, by four smaller square pools which are set somewhat deeper into the earth. In the centre of the main pool is a circular island bearing a stepped laterite shrine dedicated to the *bodhisattva* Avalokitesvara. Two intertwined serpents circle the base of the island, providing the complex with its name. To the east of the island is the sculpted figure of a horse, apparently with human legs, which seems to be swimming towards the shrine (at least during the rains, when the pond fills with water). In fact the horse, called Balaha, is a manifestation of Avalokitesvara who transformed himself into a horse to rescue a group of merchants shipwrecked off the coast of Lanka. The human legs are those of the merchants clinging to the horse, who carried them off to safety just as they were about to be captured by a sea ogress.

54

The central pool is said to represent the Himalayan Lake Anavatapta, located at the summit of the universe, which was believed to have given birth to the four great rivers of the world. These rivers are represented at Neak Pean by sculpted heads – really water-carrying gargoyle-like spouts – which, when opened, would permit water to flow from the main pool to the four smaller pools through their mouths. There are four such heads, each located in a small stone-roofed building between the main pool and the lesser square ponds. The east head represents a human being, the south head a lion, the west head a horse, and the north head an elephant. In times past pilgrims to Neak Pean would consult resident priests, then repair to the appropriate pool where servants would release a plug and allow the magical waters of the central pool to pour, via the gargoyle spouts, over the head and body of the supplicant.

The east head, a human being

The north head, an elephant

On leaving Neak Pean, the visitor should continue eastwards, along the north bank of the Jayatataka Baray, following the route of the old 'Grand Circuit'. After about 2km (1¼ miles) the road turns sharply south, following the east bank of the *baray* (former reservoir). Here a turning to the left leads to the unrestored but tranquil and charming temple of ★ **Ta Som**. Built in the late 12th century

by Jayavarman VII in honour of his father, and dedicated by him to Buddhism, the temple is in the style of the Bayon Period (*see page 43*).

Ta Som is not one of the 'great' temples of Angkor in that it is not monumental in size. What makes the temple special is its setting on the northeastern limits of the great Angkorean complex. It's off the beaten track, attracts relatively few visitors, and as a consequence is filled with birdsong and the sound of cicadas. Comprising a single shrine of one level, the temple should be entered and exited via the west gate, a cruciform *gopura* surmounted by four carved faces. The inner shrine is partly collapsed, but it is possible to walk through the covered galleries to the central sanctuary and admire the spectacular effect of the tree roots binding and clambering over the old temple buildings. It's also worth walking to the east gateway – essentially twin to the western gate, and again bearing four benignly smiling stone faces – to gaze into the silent scrublands beyond. It is probably wise to turn back at this point, however, as land mines may still be concealed in the area beyond the temple.

Ta Som and apsara

From Ta Som proceed south for about 1km (½ mile) to enter the huge East Baray. This former reservoir is now completely dry and the site of a small village called Pradak on the road to Banteay Srei and Banteay Samre (*see page 64*). In the centre of the *baray* on an artificial mound stands the temple of the ★★ **East Mebon**. This large structure is easily accessible from the road. Visitors should enter and leave by the east entrance. The temple, Hindu in origin and dedicated to the god Shiva, was founded by Rajendravarman II (941–68) in memory of his parents.

The East Mebon is impressive. One cannot help thinking how much more spectacular it must have been when the East Baray was filled with water. This huge reservoir

The East Mebon

The central and outer towers

Preah Rup

Srah Srang – the Royal Bath

2km (1¼ miles) wide by 7km (4 miles) long, must have provided a truly stunning setting for the East Mebon. It has been calculated that at the time of its construction the East Baray would have held water to an average depth of 3m (10ft), with an overall volume of 40 million cubic metres of water. Over this truly astonishing example of hydrographic engineering would have loomed the Mebon, its towers and pinnacles reflected in the still waters. Today, alas, the *baray* is almost completely dry, and the Mebon rises above rice fields.

The East Mebon is another example of an artificial temple mountain representing Mount Meru – an enduring theme of classical Khmer architecture. Surrounded by three laterite enclosure walls, the 'mountain' rises through three levels before culminating in a central platform bearing four smaller outer towers and one larger central tower. The stairways at the foot of the artificial mound are flanked by carved sandstone lions, while elephants stand astride the corners of the second and third tiers. Visitors should look at the lintel above the west *gopura*, which bears an unusual likeness to Vishnu as Narasingha, half-man and half-lion; the lintel of the north *gopura* shows Lakshmi being washed with lustral water by two elephants.

Proceeding south from the East Mebon, the road climbs out of the East Baray and, about 500m (1,600ft) from the rim of the reservoir, turns sharply to the west. On the left of the road rises a single tower called Leak Neang, and to the right is the large temple mountain of ★ **Preah Rup**. Built by Rajendravarman II just nine years after the completion of the nearby Oriental Mebon, Preah Rup is a Hindu temple dedicated to Shiva. Visitors are advised to enter and leave via the eastern gateway, the one closest to the road. Similarly, the temple mount should be climbed by the eastern stairway which is (marginally) less steep and therefore safer than the others.

Preah Rup is similar in design to the nearby East Mebon, which it overlooks. Rising, like the latter, through three levels, the central shrine is dominated by four smaller towers and one large central tower. Preah Rup differs from the Mebon, however, in that a further six large towers dominate the eastern aspect of the temple at ground level. Visitors to Preah Rup should climb to the top of the monument for excellent views north across the East Baray towards Phnom Kulen, as well as southwest where the distant spires of Angkor Wat can be readily distinguished in clear weather. The false doors on the central towers are remarkable for their craftsmanship.

On leaving Preah Rup the road heads due west past the great reservoir of **Srah Srang**, or 'Royal Bath'. This large body of water 300m (1,000ft) by 700m (2,300ft) was built on the orders of Jayavarman VII and, especially in the late afternoon and evening, makes a delightful sight as buffalos bathe in its tranquil waters. At the western side of the lake is a sandstone landing stage flanked by lions and bearing a large *garuda* on the back of a three-headed serpent. This is an excellent location to stop for a while and contemplate the waters.

Immediately behind the landing stage, further to the west, is a *gopura* in a tall laterite wall giving access to ★ **Banteay Kdei**, the 'citadel of the cells'. Constructed on the orders of the master builder Jayavarman VII, the temple was used as a Buddhist monastic complex until the mid-20th century. As a consequence, it is less overgrown than some of the other outer temples, and very pleasant to stroll through. Visitors are advised to follow the central corridor through the 'hall of the dancing girls' – so called because of a bas-relief of dancers cut into the wall – and on to the central sanctuary which contains a recent Buddha image, still much venerated by the local people. At the western end of the complex a spectacular fig tree enfolds part of the temple wall.

Banteay Kdei

57

Finally, and ideally towards the end of the day, the route leads past Banteay Kdei for about 1km (½ mile) to reach the truly spectacular temple of ★★★ **Ta Prohm** ('Ancestor of Brahma'). This very large complex was, yet again, the work of Jayavarman VII and dedicated to Buddhism. A stone stele, now removed to the Angkor Conservatory, tells us quite a lot about Ta Prohm. For example, in its prime the temple owned 3,140 villages and was maintained by 79,365 people including 18 high priests, 2,740 officials, 2,202 assistants and 615 dancers. Other statistics incised for posterity and doubtless designed to emphasise the

Ta Prohm

magnificence of the temple, as well as the wealth and power of the founder, record that Ta Prohm owned a set of gold dishes weighing more than 500kg (1,100lb), 35 diamonds, 40,620 pearls, 876 Chinese veils, 512 silk beds and 523 parasols. Alas, all have long since been lost.

Ta Prohm is a long, low complex of buildings all standing at the same level. A series of concentric galleries are connected by passages that provide shade in the heat of the day. The entire complex is surrounded by a rectangular laterite wall around 700m (2,300ft) by 1,000m (3,300ft) in length. The temple is best entered from the east via a splendid if semi-collapsed *gopura*, today filled with damaged Buddha images awaiting restoration. Beyond this is a sandstone building with particularly fine false doorways known as the 'Hall of the Dancers'. This structure, readily distinguished by its square pillars, was probably used for the performance of religious or ritual dances, in celebration of which the walls are decorated with rows of graceful *apsara*. At the time of writing it was, unfortunately, closed to visitors as it is in a state of collapse and awaiting restoration.

Apsara at Ta Prohm

The visitor should continue westwards towards the central sanctuary. This is readily identifiable because of the plainness of the stone, which is quite uncarved – probably it was formerly decorated with stucco and gilding which has perished over the years. Elsewhere there are many finely carved details, especially the delicately incised *apsara* and the elaborate *gopura*. What makes Ta Prohm so special is that, following an unusual archaeological decision, the jungle has only partly been cut back, leaving the buildings covered with the roots of huge banyan and kapok trees which rise high above the temple. Spectacular roots bind lintels and crack vaulted passageways, while parrots fly in the upper canopy and break the stillness with their shrill cries. At Ta Prohm it is easy to imagine the sense of awe that the early European explorers of Angkor must have felt.

Spectacular roots

Leave the temple via the west gateway and proceed along a shaded jungle path to cross the Siem Reap river and rejoin the 'Small Circuit'. From here one may turn north and west, passing ★ **Ta Keo** – a ziggurat-like artificial Mount Meru built by Jayavarman V (968–1001) and his successor Suryavarman I (1002–50) – and (if time and energy permit) stop briefly to visit ★ **Thommanon**. This small but impressive Hindu temple built by Suryavarman II (1113–50) is notable for its fine carvings of female divinities. From here Angkor Thom may be entered via the Victory Gate; alternatively, the road east from Ta Prohm will lead back to Banteay Kdei and route 405 to Angkor Wat and Siem Reap.

Ta Keo

Tour 3: the 'Roluos Group' of temples

Recent stupas at Lolei

The small town of Roluos, about 12km (7½ miles) south-east of Siem Reap, has given its name to the so-called 'Roluos Group' of temples which includes the earliest monuments open to visitors in the Angkor area. Roluos itself contains no monuments of any importance, though it is a colourful and picturesque enough place. Within 3km (2 miles), however, three important complexes can be found. To the north of the main Siem Reap–Phnom Penh road stand the ancient towers of Lolei, while to the south may be found the larger temples of Preah Ko and Bakong.

Some 11 centuries ago King Jayavarman II, remembered as the founder of the first unified Cambodian state, made his capital at Hariharalaya (the 'Dwelling Place of Hari-Hara', a deity combining the attributes of both Vishnu and Shiva). Today the site of Hariharalaya, the first Angkorean capital, is marked by the Roluos complex of temples, the oldest in Angkor.

Roluos can be reached by driving east along Highway 6 towards Phnom Penh or by a rather better back road from south of Siem Reap – your taxi driver will know the way.

Just before the southern turning for Roluos a dirt track leads north for several hundred metres across a usually dry reservoir, the Indratataka Baray. Not unlike the East Mebon (*see page 55*), ★ **Lolei** is situated on an artificial mound in the middle of the *baray*, which often fills with water at the height of the rainy season.

Lolei: one of the towers

Founded by King Yasovarman I (889–910), Lolei was dedicated to the Hindu deity Shiva. In style it is considered transitional between the nearby monuments of Preah Ko and Bakheng. Most people visit Lolei to view its magnificent carvings and well-preserved stone inscriptions, though the four central brick towers are somewhat tumbledown and covered with shrubbery. The temple is

Early Khmer inscriptions

Figure at Preah Ko

Restoration in progress

Bakong: the modern temple

based on a double platform rising from the *baray* and surrounded by a laterite wall. Stone lions guard the stairways leading to the main temple. Be sure to inspect the particularly fine inscriptions carved in the lintels and side posts of the false doors – they are in such an excellent state of repair that they appear almost new; only the crumbling stone at the edge of some doorways hints at their real age of around 1,000 years.

After seeing Lolei, cross Highway 6 to the south, doubling back towards Siem Reap for around 300m (1,000ft) before turning south towards the temple of ★ **Preah Ko** (the 'Sacred Bull'). Built by King Indravarman I (877–89), Preah Ko is a Hindu temple dedicated to Shiva and constructed in memory of Indravarman's parents and an earlier king, Jayavarman II, the founder of Roluos.

Preah Ko is set amid attractive rural scenery and, being somewhat off the main Angkor circuits, is usually tranquil and rarely visited. Trees provide shade – much needed in the hot season – and cream-coloured cows move slowly about eating grass. The temple, currently undergoing restoration, is in a rather dilapidated state. The walls and *gopura* of the outer enclosure have largely fallen down, but the inner enclosure is in a much better state of repair. Approaching the central area from the east, the remains of three statues of *nandi*, the sacred bull and mount of Shiva after whom the temple is named, may be seen.

The main sanctuary of Preah Ko consists of six brick towers set on a low laterite platform. Formerly each tower would have contained an image of a Hindu deity, but these have long since disappeared. The quality of the carved decorative motifs on the false doors, lintels and columns is magnificent; perhaps the carving on the east towers surpasses that on the west. Visitors should look for carvings of hanging garlands and for *kala*, mythical monstrous creatures with bulging eyes, a lion's snout, horns, clawed hands and a grinning mouth. Other monsters represented at Preah Ko are the *makara*, a large sea animal with a reptilian body and an elongated trunk-like snout, and the better-known *garuda*, a winged creature with a thick beak and prominent claws that serves as Vishnu's flying mount.

A short distance beyond Preah Ko rises the solid mass of the ★★ **Bakong**, a late 9th-century Hindu temple dedicated to the god Shiva. Today Shiva has to share the site with a modern Buddhist temple. It's worth taking a stroll around the modern temple, which has interesting if primitive murals, and is filled with friendly monks reading, chanting and often anxious to practise their English.

A thousand years ago Bakong was the central feature of Jayavarman II's capital of Hariharalaya. It is built as a temple mountain on an artificial mound surrounded by a moat and outer enclosure walls. Bakong, the largest monument of the Roluos Group, is best entered from the east by a processional way decorated with seven-headed *naga* serpents. Long, covered buildings on each side of the main eastern *gopura* were probably rest houses for pilgrims to the shrine. In the northeastern and southeastern corners of the complex stand four buildings with vents which are considered to have been crematoria. Similar buildings, which once stood in the other two corners of the complex, have collapsed.

The central part of Bakong rests on the artificial mound representing Mount Meru. This mound is surrounded by eight large brick towers – those to the west are in the best condition – which display some excellent decoration in carved sandstone. The square mound, which is something like a stepped pyramid in design, rises behind these towers in five stages, the first three of which bear carved stone elephants at the corners.

At the summit is the central sanctuary which is square, with four levels and a lotus-shaped tower in the middle. It is believed that this lotus finial was constructed at a later date, having been added to the Bakong in the 12th century, perhaps around 250 years after King Indravarman I founded the temple.

There are a number of other temples and monuments dating from the Hariharalaya period at Roluos, notably Prasat Prei Monti, Svay Pream and Prasat Trapeang Phong, but these lie farther off the beaten track and are not yet considered completely safe for visitors; land mines may still be a problem. Until they become generally accessible, it is advisable to restrict any visit to Roluos to the three main monuments described above.

61

Lotus-shaped tower

Bakong bas-relief

Washing grain at Tonlé Sap

Tour 4: Siem Reap, Banteay Srei, Banteay Samre and Tonlé Sap

Siem Reap is the base for people visiting the nearby temples of Angkor, as well the location of the nearest airport to the complex. It's engaging and comfortable with good food and accommodation. For those staying longer than three or four days, a visit to the exquisite but isolated Banteay Srei is highly recommended. For visitors who have had their fill of temples or who have time on their hands, a trip to the Vietnamese fishing village on Tonlé Sap is worthwhile.

Siem Reap (in both words the emphasis is on the last syllable) is a quiet, dusty, rather bucolic town lining the banks of the Siem Reap river, the capital of the province of the same name. Although nothing like as old as Angkor it is, nevertheless, a historic town, in indication of which its name – which translates as 'Siam defeated' – celebrates a Cambodian victory over the Siamese in pre-colonial times. The town has grown in leaps and bounds since direct flights from Bangkok were introduced, and happily it has become a more attractive and comfortable place.

Shade at Siem Reap

Fortunately Siem Reap is a pleasant place, shaded in the vicinity of the river, unpolluted by heavy traffic and with a very friendly population, many of whom speak English. Most visitors enter Siem Reap from the west having landed at the nearby international airport. The recently resurfaced road leads through paddy fields and clumps of sugar palms, passing several large new hotels in various stages of construction, before reaching the central crossroads on the left bank of the gently flowing river. To the left stands the **Grand Hotel d'Angkor**, which has recently been completely renovated by the Singapore Raffles Group. Over the years many well-known visitors to Angkor have stayed here, including such luminaries as W. Somerset Maugham,

Noel Coward, Charlie Chaplin and Jacqueline Kennedy Onassis. After watching traditional Cambodian dancers performing here during the 1920s, Maugham was moved to write: 'The beauty of these dances against the mystery of the temple made it the most unearthly and strangely beautiful sight imaginable. It was certainly more than worthwhile to have travelled thousands of miles for this, and I returned to the hotel with the exciting prospect of seeing the city and its monuments by daylight.'

Directly opposite and south of the Grand Hotel stands **King Sihanouk's Villa**, a small palace rarely visited by the reigning monarch, who seems to spend much of his time in Beijing. At the time of writing, foreign visitors to Siem Reap are permitted to walk in front of the attractive colonial-style building, though locals without appropriate business are generally shooed away.

A north turn at the central crossroads, marked by a statue of Vishnu from the nearby temple complex, leads to Angkor. The road ahead takes one to the dusty eastern district of Siem Reap with little to recommend it other than the market – best visited in the early morning for a good overview of everyday provincial Cambodian commerce.

Southwards, along the bank of the river, the road leads directly to the delightful old ★ **French Quarter**, which could just as well be in Djibouti or Algiers were it not for the Khmer sights and sounds pervading the area. There are numerous pleasant guesthouses and restaurants here, and this is certainly the best place to 'kick back' and relax during the quiet Siem Reap evenings.

French Quarter facades

Just south of the French Quarter is the recently built **New Market** (in Khmer *psar tcha*), one of the best places in town to buy souvenirs of Angkor. Some of these are cheap and unattractive, but keep an eye open for the wonderful temple-rubbings on rice paper which are most reasonably priced and look very attractive when framed. The vendors will roll them up for you and insert them in a decorated round rattan carrying case for the journey home. Superior-quality souvenirs, such as carved sandstone replicas of Angkor pieces, leather puppets and woodcarvings, may also be found at the many shops, boutiques and galleries that can be found in the Old French Quarter. Unlike the market, most of these places have fixed prices that are several times more expensive than market souvenirs – though the quality sometimes warrants the markup.

Woodcarving is a local speciality

A worthwhile Siem Reap option, particularly during the early evening, is to stroll southwards along the riverbank into the southern suburbs. Under the shady trees there are many attractive, blue-painted and decorated Cambodian stilt houses, as well as rustic bamboo **water-wheels**, some as high as 3m (10ft), which creak as they raise the waters of the Siem Reap river to irrigate the nearby rice paddies and orchards.

The justly famed temple of ★★ **Banteay Srei** lies about 30km (18 miles) northeast of Siem Reap, well beyond Angkor Wat, via an eastwards junction leading from the main 'Grand Circuit' between Prey Rup and the East Mebon. From this point it's around 20km (12 miles) to Banteay Srei, which means 'citadel of women' in Khmer. In the not-so-distant past the trip to this exceptionally beautiful temple was difficult and not particularly safe, though a large increase in visitors has meant an improved road and better security.

In the opinion of numerous experts – as well as many ordinary visitors – the temple is one of the jewels in the crown of classical Khmer statuary. Thus, while Angkor Wat, Angkor Thom and the Bayon impress, even overwhelm by their sheer size, Banteay Srei inspires through meticulous detail. It is, indeed, a scrupulously executed miniature temple complex carved in fine pink sandstone – and in the quality of the stone and the soft, almost mellifluous charm of the colour lies much of the secret of the temple's appeal. Founded in the second half of the 10th century by two Shivaite priests, the founding stele (discovered in 1936 by French archaeologist H. Marchal) tells us accurately both the date that the temple was completed – 967AD – and the names of its founders.

Classical Khmer statuary at Banteay Srei

The temple of Banteay Srei is of rectangular design, enclosed by three walls and the remains of a moat. The visitor is advised to enter by the main entrance on the east side, through a cross-shaped laterite gateway decorated with a carving of Indra on a three-headed elephant. Proceed for about 80m (260ft) along a processional way decorated with warm, pink sandstone pillars, then through another decorated gateway bearing a likeness of 'Sita being abducted by Ravana' and you will reach the central temple complex.

The central complex consists of a number of structures including, most importantly, shrines dedicated to Shiva (the central and southern buildings) and to Vishnu (the northern building). The shrines are guarded by beautifully worked figures, many sadly damaged. The situation is not as bad as it may seem as many of the best figurines were taken away to be stored in Phnom Penh. Side panels, too, which have disappeared and been replaced by plain laterite are safe, but in the Musée Guimet in Paris. No doubt the Cambodian authorities will seek their return at some time, though whether this French example of 'Elginism' can eventually be undone remains to be seen.

The main themes represented in the many elaborately carved lintels and frontons of Banteay Srei are derived from the Hindu epic, the *Ramayana*. Watch for likenesses of the heroes and heroines (Shiva, Parvati, the monkeys of Hanuman, Krishna) and the arch-demon Ravana, most easily distinguished by his evil visage, multiple heads and arms. Also worthy of note are the finely carved figures of male and female divinities set in recessed niches of the central towers. The style – classified by art historians as 'Banteay Srei style' – shows the female divinities with plaits or buns, wearing simple, loosely draped skirts and sporting a wealth of jewellery. The male divinities, by contrast, carry lances and wear simple loincloths.

Elaborate carving

On the return journey to Siem Reap, the visitor should enter the East Baray, but instead of turning west towards Angkor should turn east and, leaving the Baray, drive approximately 500m (¼ mile) along a rough dirt track to **Banteay Samre** ('Citadel of Samre'). This temple is well off the beaten track, and while apparently safe it is advised not to walk off the track or beyond the outer walls of the main complex because of possible land mines.

Roughly square in plan, Banteay Samre is a massive, heavy structure that differs markedly from the almost ethereal Banteay Srei. The name Samre is thought to refer to a minority ethnic group who lived in the region of Phnom Kulen to the north of Angkor, though their relationship to this particular temple remains unclear. There are no known inscriptions relating to the temple, but the style suggests 12th to 13th century, which is the same period as Angkor Wat. A solid, high laterite wall surrounds the temple, with entrances at the four cardinal points. Inside, uniquely, there is a laterite-paved moat which must have appeared splendid when filled with water; alas, today it is dry. The main temple complex is reached by a raised laterite causeway. The visitor should look for serpent balustrades on the stairs leading to the moats. These represent the multi-headed *naga* Muchalinda who sheltered the meditating Buddha from the rain.

65

A particularly worthwhile excursion from Siem Reap lies south on the nearby ★ **Tonlé Sap**, Cambodia's great lake. The road leads south from town towards Phnom Krom, the only hill in an otherwise flat landscape. **Phnom Krom** – which is gradually being quarried away – is surmounted by a 10th-century sandstone temple of the same name, which may be reached by a long flight of steps. The climb, while tiring, is well worth it for the view over the nearby lake and north towards Siem Reap town.

Phnom Krom was founded by King Yasovarman I (889–910), and is dedicated to the Hindu trinity of Shiva, Vishnu and Brahma. The scenery varies greatly from season to season, as during the rains the Tonlé Sap expands considerably (*see page 6*). In consequence, the last several kilometres of road run along a narrow causeway leading to the 'port' for Battambang, Kampong Chnnang and Phnom Penh.

On the shores of Tonlé Sap

At the end of the causeway is a small, rather malodorous fishing village. For five to ten dollars an hour, one can hire a boat to explore the nearby **'floating village'**. Be sure to choose a boat with a good roof as a sun-shield, especially during the hot season. The sun, already fierce, is reflected by the still waters of Tonlé Sap, and can prove very trying, and a sunscreen and hat are recommended.

At least an hour is needed to see the 'floating village' (in fact something of a misnomer, as many of the houses are built on tall stilts, especially nearer the shore). It's a fascinating experience, and provides some unusual photo opportunities. Along the shore most villagers seem to be Khmer, but further out in an extended area of houseboats the people are Vietnamese. One way of distinguishing is to look for the Chinese characters and small red altars characteristic of Vietnamese homes. Another is to watch for the *non la*, or conical hats worn by Vietnamese women everywhere to protect their complexions.

The floating village

66

The 'village' consists of a fairly wide main thoroughfare, with narrow passages between houseboats, stilt houses and extensive fish traps. The water isn't deep – in the dry season it would be possible to stand in some places – but it is immensely rich in silt and sediment, so that the propellers of the boats look almost as though they are churning warm chocolate. The people clearly aren't rich, but their unusual community has all kinds of unexpected amenities. There's a police station, a couple of floating petrol stations, fish farms – you are likely to be taken to visit one of these and offered a cold drink – even floating restaurants and, amazingly, pigsties. Men fish and repair vessels or extend their houses, women cook and wash up in kitchens invariably at the stern of the boats, and children play on the wooden decks and landings, or swim in the muddy waters of the lake.

Route 6

Preah Vihear is once more open to visitors

The 'lost' temple complex of Preah Vihear

Kantharalak – Preah Vihear *See map on page 68*

Perched on a high cliff on the edge of the Dongrak Escarpment overlooking Cambodia, Preah Vihear (known to the Thais as Khao Phra Viharn) is remarkable both for its outstanding Khmer architecture and for its stunning location. Long claimed by both Thailand and Cambodia, the temple complex was finally awarded to the latter by the World Court in 1963, though the question of ownership still rankles with many Thais. Whatever the case, for the foreseeable future the only practical way of access – short of climbing hundreds of feet up a sheer and treacherous rock face – will remain via the province of Sisaket, in Thailand's remote northeast.

Local sugar palm fruits

Possible bases for the exploration of Preah Vihear are the northeastern Thai cities of Surin, Sisaket and Ubon Ratchathani. Both Surin and Sisaket, and nearby Buriram, are home to Thailand's one million plus population of Khmer speakers. Ubon Ratchathani, by contrast, is overwhelmingly Thai Lao in its citizenship. All three towns have adequate accommodation, though only Surin and Ubon have first-class hotels. An alternative would be to stay in the small Thai town of **Kantharalak**, just 30km (18 miles) from Preah Vihear, which has one comfortable air-conditioned hotel, the Kantharalak Palace. Preah Vihear is best visited as a day trip, setting out early by bus, or better still in a hired car or taxi from Surin or Ubon. Make sure you leave as early as possible, for the temple site is large. At the time of writing, the complex (and the Thai-Cambodian frontier) closes at 4pm. Preah Vihear

is a major temple, one of the great sights of the region, and at least one day is required to do it justice. Visitors should consider taking a packed lunch with them, as no restaurants or even foodstalls exist across the frontier in Cambodia. Cold drinks are widely available.

A monks' outing

The frontier-straddling temple of ★★ **Preah Vihear** is historically Khmer and therefore should logically be attached to Cambodia for reasons of cultural heritage, although its inaccessibility from the Cambodian side makes the World Court's decision seem somewhat inappropriate.

Closed for decades because of civil war and general brigandage, Preah Vihear opened briefly between 1991 and 1993, only to become off-limits again due to the presence of Khmer Rouge forces in the region. Then, in August 1998, following the death of Pol Pot and the expulsion of the Khmer Rouge from its nearby base at Anglong Veng, the temple opened once more – hopefully, this time, for good. Foreign (non-Thai) visitors to Preah Vihear must pay a 400 baht entry fee per head and deposit their passports with the Thai border police.

Enjoying the view

The new road from Kantharalak to the temple stops abruptly at the Thai frontier, and visitors must proceed on foot across a rocky plateau, down a steep embankment, and then up a long slope to the initial – steep and tricky – temple steps. It's not a climb for the old or unfit, though many elderly Thai pilgrims, tiny old women prominent among them, pull themselves to the top of the hill. Such Thai visitors often complain bitterly about the damage to the site, assuring all who listen that – were the temple still in Thai hands – things would be different.

Vendor at the temple

Preah Vihear is an extraordinary place, possibly the most impressive Khmer historical site after Angkor. Although in sad need of restoration, the temple is magnificent, and one is left wondering how the original builders managed

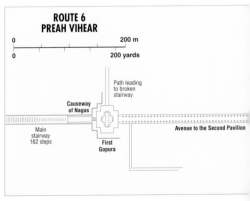

**ROUTE 6
PREAH VIHEAR**

0   200 m
0   200 yards

Path leading to broken stairway

Causeway of Nagas

Avenue to the Second Pavilion

Main stairway 162 steps

First Gopura

to transport such massive blocks of stone to the peak of the Dongrak escarpment – a height of 600m (1,950ft). In fact, Preah Vihear took around two centuries to build, starting during the reign of Rajendravarman II in the mid-10th century and reaching completion during the reign of Surayavarman II in the early 12th century. It was the latter monarch, truly a visionary builder, who also began the construction of Angkor Wat. It is thought that the site of the temple had long been holy to the Khmers, who are believed to have revered the locality for at least 500 years before the building of Preah Vihear.

Constructed in the Baphuon and early Angkor styles, Preah Vihear was built originally as a Hindu temple dedicated to the god Shiva. Of the four main *gopura*, or elaborately decorated gateways, the first two are in serious disrepair, though fine examples of carving – *apsaras*, divinities – are still visible. The third *gopura* is comparatively well preserved, with a finely carved lintel depicting Shiva and his consort Uma sitting on Nandi, the bull.

Gopura detail

The temple extends for around 900m (3,000ft), through five separate stages, before culminating in the massive bulk of the main sanctuary perched high on the cliff top. Here the great *prasat* has been thrown to the ground – perhaps by an earthquake – and mighty blocks of carved stone lie in a tumbled heap, awaiting eventual restoration. Everywhere there are signs warning visitors not to stray off the sanctioned paths, for the danger of land mines is very real.

The temple is now firmly under the control of the Cambodian army, and young soldiers – some little more than children – watch silently as a regular stream of Thai and other visitors pick their way over the stones. Once through the main temple complex, head for the nearby cliff top and gaze across the Cambodian plains, so near but so inaccessible. It would be easy to fall, but any other sort of descent is all but impossible.

A soldier patrols

69

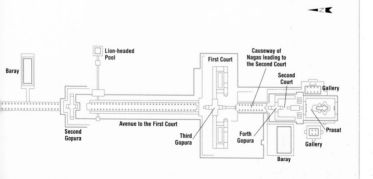

Architectural Heritage

Opposite: faces of Angkor

From an architectural perspective, Cambodia is something of an enigma. Home to possibly the greatest and certainly the oldest high civilisation in mainland Southeast Asia, the country is studded with unique and outstandingly beautiful temple complexes, both Hindu and Buddhist, dating from the 6th to the 15th centuries AD. Modern temple architecture, it must be said, is a disappointment by comparison, though due allowance must be made for the systematic destruction and desecration wrought by the icon-oclastic Khmer Rouge regime between 1975 and 1979.

Perhaps because King Sihanouk was in residence under effective house arrest during much of this period, the Royal Palace and Silver Pagoda at Phnom Penh were spared. Elsewhere, however, Buddha statues were decapitated, blown up or hurled into rivers, and temples and mosques were turned into grain storage barns or pigsties. Christian monuments did not fare any better: Phnom Penh Cathedral was levelled, and even the gods of Mammon were not spared as the National Bank was blown up. Fortunately, however, there were limits to even the Khmer Rouge regime's iconoclasm. Angkor and the other wonders of ancient Khmer civilisation were either protected or ignored and left to the encroaching jungle. Not for nothing has an image of Angkor Wat appeared on the flags of Cambodian regimes of all political persuasions. The great temple complex is a potent image of national identity which has and continues to transcend politics.

Silver Pagoda in Phnom Penh

Bayon detail

Temple architecture

The temple architecture of ancient Khmer civilisation, both Hindu and subsequently Buddhist, is unique in style and readily identifiable. Building materials include laterite (often as a plinth or base), surmounted by structures of sandstone and/or stucco-covered brick. Elaborately carved sandstone lintels feature scenes from the Hindu pantheon, commonly the churning of the primaeval ocean of milk or Vishnu reclining on a lotus flower. The *Ramayana* and, from around 1200AD, scenes from the Buddhist *jataka* (life cycles), illuminate bas-reliefs of extraordinary quality. Everywhere, too, there are exquisitely executed figures of *apsara* (heavenly dancing girls), bearing a wealth of jewellery and elaborate headdresses.

The central feature of the classical Khmer temple is often a stylised representation of Mount Meru of Hindu mythology. Main entranceways – with a few exceptions, notably at Angkor Wat itself – are from the east, marked by elaborately decorated *gopura* (gateways). Windows are all but filled with rows of finely turned stone balusters. The central temple complex, usually set within several

Bas-relief with rishi (ascetics) at Preah Khan

concentric enclosure walls, is generally characterised by the presence (in Hindu temples) of *linga* (stylised male phalli) and their counterpart, the female *yoni*. In times past lustral water was poured over *linga* and *yoni*, often conjoined, before being used as a source of blessing and purification. Statues of the major Hindu deities Shiva, Vishnu and Brahma are often present.

Other commonly represented figures from the Hindu pantheon included Nandi, the bull mount of Shiva, and the garuda, or bird-king mount of Vishnu. Other gods include Parvati or Uma, the wife of Shiva, their sons Skanda, the God of War, and the elephant-headed Ganesh, the God of Knowledge. An interesting and particularly Khmer deity, Hari-Hara, represents a composite of Shiva and Vishnu. Subsequently, as Buddhism gradually replaced Hinduism from around the 11th century, images of the Buddha and scenes from the ever-popular *Ramayana* were used in temple consecration and decoration.

Buddhist temples built in and after the 19th century are altogether less imposing affairs, though artistic merit is not always lacking. The influence of neighbouring Thailand is clearly dominant, though few contemporary Cambodian wat can match up to their Thai counterparts. The Royal Palace, too, is consciously based on the Thai court in Bangkok, and was indeed constructed under the supervision of French architects. It is, nevertheless, a fine complex and forms a fitting heart to the royal city of Phnom Penh.

Other landmarks

Other buildings of note in the Cambodian capital include the rust-red, traditionally styled National Museum and a plethora of early 20th-century French colonial architecture, particularly in the former French quarter to the north and west of Wat Phnom. Similar concentrations of French colonial architecture can be found in most provincial capitals, notably at Siem Reap, Kompông Cham, Battambang and Kâmpôt. Although often sadly run down, they are gradually being restored and repainted as Cambodia continues to pick itself up from the ashes.

The presence of Cham Muslims in Cambodian towns from Siem Reap to Sihanoukville (Kompông Som) means that mosques and minarets form a perhaps unexpected part of the skyline. By and large they are unremarkable imitations of the Islamic architectural style common in parts of the South Asian subcontinent and the Malay-Indonesian archipelago. To the north of Phnom Penh, however, some interestingly unorthodox mosques, generally painted in the preferred Cham colour of pale blue in contrast to the traditional Islamic green, have been erected in the wake of Khmer Rouge persecution.

Ramayana mural at the Silver Pagoda

National Museum

Colonial influence in Kâmpôt

Music, Literature and Dance

Music

There are two types of traditional orchestra in Cambodia, the all-male *pip hat* and the all-female *mohori*. Both comprise 11 traditional musical instruments. These include stringed instruments, flutes, gongs, xylophones and three-stringed guitars. Music is sometimes accompanied by song, either improvised ballads or formal court chants. At some festivals a traditional orchestra (*phleng pinpeat*) will give performances of royal court music. Another type of orchestra is the *phleng khmer*, which usually performs at weddings. Popular music has been strongly influenced in recent years by both Thai and Chinese pop culture.

Pip hat percussionists

Literature

As in neighbouring Indianised countries like Thailand, Burma and Laos, much traditional Cambodian literature revolves around the great Hindu epic, the *Ramayana*, known in its Khmer version as the *Reamker*. This describes the story of Prince Rama, an incarnation of Vishnu, and his wife Sita who is kidnapped by Ravana, the demon-king of Lanka. The story is more than 2,000 years old, and figures prominently in the bas-reliefs at Angkor.

73

Dance

The Cambodian Royal Ballet, once celebrated by such luminaries as the sculptor Auguste Rodin and the writer W. Somerset Maugham, suffered particularly badly under the Khmer Rouge regime, which almost succeeded in wiping it out. Fortunately one or two dancers survived, as did Princess Bupphadevi, favourite daughter of King Sihanouk, in exile in France. The Royal Ballet has been painstakingly rebuilt, and today performances can be seen at the Hotel Cambodiana and elsewhere in Phnom Penh. Classical Khmer dance (*lamthon*) as performed by the Royal Ballet bears a striking resemblance to that of the Thai royal court. Training takes many years, and sumptuously elaborate costumes and headdresses are worn. It's a real spectacle that should not be missed. Cambodian masked theatre (*khaul*) features classical dances depicting incidents from the Buddhist life cycle stories (*jataka*).

Cambodian Royal Ballet

Elaborate costume

Shadow puppets

Cambodians have a tradition of shadow puppetry called *nang sbaek thom* (shadow plays). These are narrated by actors concealed below the puppet screen. A light behind them casts images of the puppets on the screen for the audience to watch. The puppets are made of cow or buffalo hide and can be very intricate. Siem Reap is considered by many to be the home of this art form.

Water throwing during Chaul Chnam (Cambodian New Year)

Burning spirit money at Chinese New Year

Festivals

There is a wide range of festivals and secular public holidays in Cambodia reflecting the nation's diverse cultural and ethnic backgrounds, as well as the drastic changes of regime that have taken place over the past three decades. Most religious festivals find their inspiration in the Buddhist tradition, and closely parallel festivals held in neighbouring Thailand and Laos. Other festivals – notably Chinese New Year, which is the same as Vietnamese *Tet* – are rooted in Sinitic or Mahayana traditions.

January/February
7 January: National Day celebrates the overthrow of the Khmer Rouge regime by the Vietnamese with Cambodian rebel assistance in 1979–80.

Celebration of Chinese Lunar New Year and Vietnamese New Year (*Tet*): there are sizeable communities of Chinese and Vietnamese in Phnom Penh and other cities and many shops close for three days. Although the exploding of firecrackers is banned in Vietnam, it is still possible to witness this spectacle in Vietnamese-settled parts of Cambodia.

Full moon: *Magha Bochea* celebrates the gathering of 1,200 disciples to witness the Buddha's last sermon.

1 February: Friendship Day celebrates the Friendship Treaty between Vietnam and Cambodia, signed in 1980.

March
8 March: International Women's Day when processions with floats are held in most towns.

April
13–15 April: *Chaul Chnam* (Cambodian New Year), a three-day festival around the middle of the month. It

involves a lot of water throwing. Offerings are made at temples, and houses are cleaned. This is a time of year for many overseas Khmers to return home. Children build miniature sand stupas in representation of Mount Meru.

May
1 May: International Workers' Day.
9 May: Genocide Day to commemorate the victims of the Khmer Rouge.
Mid to late May: *Bon Choat Preah Nengkal* (Ploughing of the Holy Furrow) marks the beginning of the rice-planting season. It is usually led by the royal family and was originally a Hindu rite. The sacred oxen are offered various foods to eat by the Brahmin priests, and from their choice – beans, maize, rice, etc – the bountifulness of the coming harvest can be predicted.
Full moon: *Vesak Buchea* commemorates the Buddha's birth, enlightenment and entry into Nirvana.

June
19 June: Armed Forces' Day.

July
Beginning of *Chol Vassa* (Buddhist Lent), an auspicious time for young Cambodian males to join the monkhood.

Monks doing the rounds

September/October/November
Bon Kathen (end of Buddhist Lent), a 29-day festival during which offerings are made to ancestors, monks are given new robes and other offerings by devout Buddhists and those wishing to accrue merit.
Late September: *Bon Dak Ben* (Spirit Commemoration Festival), a 15-day festival culminating at full moon in *Bon Prachum Ben*, the Cambodian equivalent of All Soul's Day. Ancestors are remembered and respects are paid through offerings at temples throughout the country.
Bon Om Tuk (Water Festival), celebrating the beginning of the cool dry season. The current in the Tonlé Sap river reverses at this time of the year and begins to empty into the Mekong. In Phnom Penh boat races are held and monks at temples around the country will row ceremonial boats.
31 October: King Sihanouk's Birthday is celebrated with a spectacular show of fireworks by the Royal Palace.
9 November: Independence Day (marking independence from France in 1953) and Khmer National Day. There are grand parades in front of the Royal Palace with floats, bands and banners highlighting Cambodia's achievements.

Balloon vendor in Phnom Penh

December
2 December: National Reconstruction Day.
10 December: International Human Rights Day.

Food and Drink

Cambodian cuisine, though uniquely Khmer, draws heavily on the traditions of both its Thai neighbours and Chinese residents. An oft-repeated generalisation, which is nevertheless pretty accurate, likens Cambodian food to Thai food, but without the spiciness. The main national staple is of course rice, but French colonial influence has dictated that the Cambodians eat more bread – generally French-style baguettes – than any other Southeast Asian country. Because of the country's incredible richness in waterways, including the Mekong, Sap and Bassac rivers, not to mention the Tonlé Sap, freshwater fish and prawns are especially popular – in addition to which plenty of fresh seafood is available from the Gulf of Thailand. Beef, pork, chicken, duck and other poultry are widely available but generally more expensive than fish dishes. Other less well-known Cambodian delicacies include locusts, field rats, snakes and land crabs.

Fish at O Russei Market

Soup is served as an accompaniment to almost all Cambodian meals, though it is always with the main dishes, not before as in the West. Some of the better-known soup dishes include *somlar machou banle* (sour fish soup), *somlar machou bangkang* (sour and spicy prawn soup, akin to Thai *tom yam gung*), *somlar chapek* (pork soup with ginger) and *mon sngor* (chicken and coriander soup). *Num banh choc* (rice noodle and fish soup) is a common and popular breakfast.

Crusty rice and curry sauce

77

Other common Cambodian dishes include *khao poun* (rice noodles in a coconut-based sauce), *hamok* (fish with coconut milk steamed in a banana leaf), *sach mon chha khnhei* (stir-fried chicken with ginger), *somlar machou sachko* (sour beef stew) and *choeeng chomni chrouc chean* (fried pork spareribs). *An sam chruk* (pork and soybeans marinated in ginger and chilli) can be delicious, but packs a fairly hefty punch. Similarly, watch out for *pong tea kon* (fertilised duck egg containing an embryo, like the Filipino *balut*) which is not to everybody's taste.

Many dishes are served *trey*, or grilled. Thus *trey aing* (grilled fish) is available just about everywhere, as is *trey chean neung spey* (fried fish with vegetables). By extension, *trey mon* is grilled chicken, *trey sachko* is grilled beef, and so on. Fish and meat dishes not served with noodles are generally accompanied by rice. Indispensable condiments – certainly as far as the Cambodians are concerned – are *prahoc* (fish sauce just like Thai *nam pla* and Vietnamese *nuoc mam*) and *tuk trey* (fish sauce with ground, roasted peanuts added).

Travellers up country will generally find themselves limited to Cambodian cuisine, or to the fairly ubiquitous baguette and pâté. In towns of any size – all provincial

Baguette and pâté cart

Chinese food is widely available

capitals, for example – Chinese food is widely available, generally reflecting the southern coastal origin of most of Cambodia's Overseas Chinese migrants. Expect, therefore, Cantonese, Hokkien, Teochou and Hailam fare, but don't waste your time looking for Szechuan or Yunnanese cuisine. In the west of the country, notably at Poipet, Sisophon, Battambang and Siem Reap, Thai cuisine is widespread. Similarly in the east, at Kâmpôt, Takeo, Kompông Cham and Svay Rieng, Vietnamese culinary influence is common. Sihanoukville (Kompông Som) excels at seafood cooked in every conceivable way, and also has a fast-growing smattering of western food outlets – French, Italian, British, German and Australian.

Phnom Penh has, naturally enough, the widest range of restaurants in the country. Here the visitor can find everything listed above as well as Greek, Turkish, North Indian, South Indian, Malay and – increasingly – fast-food restaurants. The capital also serves some of the best French food available in Indochina, as well as some unexpected colonial hangovers from the Middle East and North Africa, notably cous-cous and *merguez*, spicy Moroccan sausage.

Fruit

There is an abundance of fruit in Cambodia. In the appropriate seasons – especially towards the end of the hot season in May – the markets overflow with a wide variety of exotic fruits. There's fruit to be had the year round, though, and it's generally both reasonably priced and (if carefully washed) healthy and safe. Among the most popular and widespread are mango, coconut, rambutan, durian, mangosteen, starfruit, pineapple, watermelon and a wide variety of bananas.

Ubiquitous watermelon

Drinks

It's always best to drink bottled water in Cambodia. The traveller should also beware of ice of unknown provenance, particularly up country or at street stalls. Soft drinks like cola and lemonade manufactured by internationally known companies are available everywhere, as is canned and bottled beer.

Refreshment is at hand

International beers to look for are Carlsberg, Heineken, Tiger, ABC, Victoria Bitter, Fosters, San Miguel and Singha; local brands include Angkor, Angkor Stout and Bayon. Draft Angkor is available in Phnom Penh, Sihanoukville and Siem Reap. Imported wine – shades of Cambodia's colonial past – is similarly available in major towns, and domestic varieties promising strength and virility are widespread.

Caution should be exercised with fresh fruit juices and sugar cane juice, but cartons and cans of fruit juice, milk and drinking yoghurt are available on supermarket shelves in the capital and at Sihanoukville. Coffee – often very good – and tea are available throughout the country.

Restaurant selection

This selection from Cambodia's principal centres is listed according to the following categories: $$$ = expensive; $$ = moderate; $ = cheap.

Phnom Penh

Café Manivong, Hotel Le Royal, 92 Rukhak Vithei Duan Penh. An elegant brasserie with an excellent daily buffet. $$$. **Boddhi Tree**, 50, Street 107 (opposite Toul Sleng Museum). Delicious Khmer food in a charming old wooden house that also serves as a guesthouse. $. **Baan Thai**, No 2, Street 306, Good Thai food in a relaxed setting. $. **Bayon Hotel and Restaurant**, No 2, Street 75 (near French Embassy). Some of the best French food in town. $$. **Cantina**, 347 Sisowath Quay. Great Mexican food and American dishes with an engaging view of the riverside street scene. $$. **Cambodia Club**, Sisowath Quay and Street 178. This open-air riverside restaurant has a good selection of pizza. $. **Chiang Mai**, 227 Sisowath Quay. Reasonably priced Thai food with sidewalk seating on the riverfront. $. **Foreign Correspondence Club of Cambodia** (FCCC), 363 Sisowath Quay. Easily the most atmospheric restaurant in Phnom Penh. Magical views of the river and National Museum compliment the excellent international menu. $$. **Frizz**, 335 Sisowath Quay. Riverfront restaurant specialising in Khmer cuisine. $$. **The Globe**, Sisowath Quay. European and Khmer food served in a beautiful old building overlooking the river and park. $$. **Ginga**, 295 Manivong. Phnom Penh's most popular Japanese restaurant. $$. **Irina**, No 7, Street 228. Authentic and tasty Russian food in a placid old villa. $$. **La Croisette**, Sisowath

Restaurant at the FCCC

Mixed menu

Riverfront café

Le Tonkin

Quay. Newly opened French and Khmer restaurant along the riverfront. $$. **La Reine du Mekong**, located dockside. This floating restaurant is actually a converted double-decker wooden riverboat, and cruises nightly from 5pm to 7pm. $$. **Le Tonkin**, Samdech Sothearos Boulevard, close to the National Assembly. Fine Vietnamese cuisine in a comfortable setting. $$. **Le Bistro**, No 4, Street 29, French restaurant in a colonial villa. Seating in the leafy garden is also available. $$. **Lucky Burger**, 160 Sihanouk, next to the Lucky Market. Good burgers and fries, and other fast food options. $. **Lyon D'Or**, 12, Street 110. Reasonably priced French specialties as well as Khmer dishes. $$. **Mount Everest**, 98 Sihanouk. A relaxed place with Nepalese and Indian specialties. $. **Nouveau Pho de Paris**, 26 Manivong. This restaurant has an excellent selection of Vietnamese, Chinese and Khmer dishes. $. **Pon Lok**, 319–232 Sisowath Quay. Overlooking the Sap River, this authentic Khmer restaurant is very popular with locals. $$. **Topaz**, 102 Sotheraos Boulevard, near Hong Kong Centre. Popular with Phnom Penh's international community. Serves excellent Thai and French food. $$. **Eid's**, 216, Street 51. Serves some very good Khmer and Thai food. $.

Continental

Bayon

Siem Reap

Angkor Café, opposite Angkor Wat. Excellent Khmer food and European pastries in an unparalleled setting. $$$. **Apsara Restaurant and Theatre**, opposite Angkor Village. Nightly traditional dance performances and set Khmer menu. $$. **Bamboo House**, east bank of river. Filipino dishes done with more flair than anything you'll find in the Philippines. $. **Bayon**, just off Route 6. Standard Khmer food and western breakfasts. $. **Blue Pumpkin**, opposite the hospital. Hugely popular due to excellent pasta, salads and fresh baked breads. $$. **Continental Café**, old French Quarter, next to the river. A varied European menu amid colonial atmosphere. $$. **Dead Fish Tower**, Sivatha Boulevard. With architecture as playful as its name implies, this restaurant offers good Khmer and Thai food. $$. FCC **Angkor**, Pokambor Street. A new branch of the famous Phnom Penh Foreign Correspondents Club. Food and ambience almost match the original. $$. **Kokoon**, near the Old Market. Sandwiches and fruit smoothies make this a convenient place for a light lunch before exploring the ruins. $$. **Les Orientalistes**, Wat Bo Street. Fine French and Khmer cuisine in an imaginatively designed setting. $$$. **Little India**, near the Old Market. Siem Reap's oldest and best Indian restaurant. $. **Lotus**, in front of the Psar Tcha market. European food popular with visitors. $$. **Mandalay Inn**, Sivatha Boulevard. An eclectic mix of Khmer and Burmese dishes. $.

Sign of the Lotus

Monorom, Sivatha Boulevard, near the Zanzybar Pub. Geared towards Asian package tourists, the Chinese food is good and reasonably priced. $$. **Red Piano**, near the Old Market. One of the most popular places on town for both food and drinks. Extensive wine list. $$. **Tell Restaurant**, Sivatha Boulevard. European food with an emphasis on German dishes. $$.

Sihanoukville (Kampong Som)
Angkor Arms, Ekareach Street. Traditional English pub. $. **Bungalow Village**, on the waterfront. A great view of the ocean to go with the western breakfasts, Khmer and Thai food. $. **Casablanca**, near Samudera Market. Vegetarian food and cocktails in a friendly, used bookstore. $. **Hawaii Seaview**, South Victory Beach. Beachside seating gives this seafood restaurant a relaxed ambience. $$. **Holy Cow**, near the bus station. Guesthouse restaurant with good sandwiches, soups and salads. $. **Marlin Bar and Grill**, Ekareach Street. Barbecued steaks and draught beer are excellent here. $$. **Mrs. Sam's**, Weather Station Hill. Long-running restaurant with filling western breakfasts, Khmer food and sunset views. $. **Snake House**, Victory Beach. This Russian-managed place has excellent European food set amidst Cambodia's only reptile house. $$. **Susaday**, Ochheuteal Beach Street. French and Khmer cuisine near the beach. $. **Yin-Yang**, Victory beach. German-run establishment with good German food and a beer-swilling monkey for entertainment. $.

Shopping

Gems and jewellery
Pailin, Cambodia's major source of gemstones, was pretty much worked out over the past 20 years by the Khmer Rouge, who exported the stones to Thailand. Even today it remains the fiefdom of former KR leader Ieng Sary, and therefore well off most tourist itineraries. Gems and jewellery are available, however, at the Central Market and Tuol Tom Pong Market in Phnom Penh.

Silver
Cambodia produces some very fine silver filigree work, as well as silver belts, jewellery and figurines. Many of the silversmiths are Cham Muslims, working in villages north of Phnom Penh. Good places to look for silver include the Central Market, Tuol Tom Pong Market and the handicraft shop at the Royal Palace.

Antiques and Pseudo-Antiques
In Phnom Penh, head for Tuol Tom Pong Market. At Siem Reap try the shops around the Angkor Conservatory, the

Carved apsaras at Tuol Tom Pong Market

81

Browsing at O Russei Market

New Market south of the former French Quarter, and Baray Tucville near the airport. High-quality wood and stone carvings are available, as are attractively worked metal heads of Jayavarman VII. Authentic antiquities from Angkor should not be purchased under any circumstances.

Silk

Takêo province, south of Phnom Penh, is the silk weaving centre of Cambodia, but you will find family weaving ventures all over the country. Purchase long lengths of silk to take home, or have them made up at one of the many reasonably priced tailor shops. An alternative is to purchase one of the beautifully woven silk *kramaa* (scarves), which have become synonymous with Khmer cultural identity.

Books

The best place to buy books is the capital, Phnom Penh. Monument Books, on Monivong Boulevard, has an unrivalled collection of Cambodiana, and the first-floor bookshop of the Foreign Correspondents Club is worth a visit.

Nightlife

Cambodia cannot be recommended as a nightlife destination. Although security is improving, there still remains a risk of robbery. Nightlife in Phnom Penh is cyclic. Government crackdowns have periodically shut the venues down, but inevitably the discos, nightclubs and karaoke bars always reopen. There is limited nightlife at both Siem Reap and Sihanoukville (Kompông Som). Don't carry large sums of money and take a taxi back to your hotel.

Phnom Penh
Elephant Bar, 92 Rukhak Vithei Daun Penh (off Monivong Boulevard), tel: 023-981 888. A classy bar in the world-famous Le Royal Hotel. Dress accordingly. There are many Karaoke bars in town. **Mega Club**, 37, Street 282, is one of the longest-lasting and best-known of these.

Siem Reap
Ivy Bar, near the Old Market. Relaxed and friendly with some colonial ambience.
Martini, at the southern end of town. Open garden restaurant and bar area with an attached disco.
Zanzybar, Sivutha Street, near the Bakheng Hotel. Opens early evening and closes very late. A good place to finish off a long day.

Sihanoukville (Kompông Som)
Le Cyree, Sopheakmongkol Street. A Southeast Asian watering hole of the old school.

On the floor in Siem Reap

Active Holidays

On the green at the Cambodia Golf Club

Cambodia isn't really an appropriate place for 'action holidays', at least not yet. Trekking, for example, in a land still plagued by the curse of land mines, does not seem a very sensible option, though the Cambodian authorities are seeking to promote the remote upland provinces of Mondulkiri and Rattanakiri as future eco-tourism paradises for trekkers and naturalists. Both provinces are currently open for adventurous tourists, but Ratanakiri is far more accessible. The easiest way to get there is to fly to Ban Lung, though boating up the Mekong to Stung Treng is an alternative. Those deciding to visit the northeast should take a few extras such as mosquito repellent, favourite snacks, some items for the locals (pencils and pads of paper for the village schools) and reading material.

Elephant trekking in Mondulkiri Province

The dangers of mines and bandits mean that really only the coast offers appropriate action activities. Here, though, the options are safe and expanding fast. At Sihanoukville (Kompông Som) snorkelling, diving, water-skiing, wind-surfing and fishing are the main attractions. Hang-gliding – as in the Thai resort of Pattaya – is also becoming popular. Kep, by contrast, remains under-developed at present, though in future this attractive seaside resort is likely to regain its former status as a playground for international travellers and Phnom Penh's elite.

In Sihanoukville (Kompông Som) the places to go for watersport activities include **EcoSea Dive** (tel: 012-654 104), where motor boats can be hired for snorkelling, diving and visiting offshore islands; **Chez Claude** (tel: 012-824 870), which can organise diving and fishing trips in the waters off Sihanoukville aboard a local wooden fishing vessel; and **Canoeing Cambodia** (012-870 993) for paddling trips to Snake Island (Ko Pos).

Getting There

By plane

Cambodia is served by several regional airlines. These international flights land at Phnom Penh's Pochentong Airport and Siem Reap Airport. At the moment Pochentong is unable to accept long-haul flights, though there are plans to upgrade the airport. Regional airports serving international flights from Europe and the United States include Bangkok, Ho Chi Minh City, Kuala Lumpur, Hong Kong and Singapore. There are daily flights between Bangkok and Phnom Penh with Thai International Airways and Bangkok Airways. Also there are daily flights from Ho Chi Minh City with Vietnam Airlines. Singapore provides daily connections through Silk Air. Less frequently there are flights from Vientiane (Lao Aviation), Hong Kong (Dragonair) and Kuala Lumpur (Malaysia Airlines).

Royal Air Cambodge

Bangkok Airways handles daily flights to Siem Reap, and this is the most popular route to Angkor. During the November to February high season it's best to book in advance via the Internet (www.bangkokair.com). It is advisable to reconfirm all your flights 72 hours before take-off. A departure tax (US$20) is levied for all international flights.

85

Pochentong Airport is 10km (6 miles) from the centre of Phnom Penh and the journey into town takes around 20 minutes. Taxis and motorcycle taxis can be hired in front of the main terminal building. At the time of writing, the average fare to Phnom Penh centre is US$5 by taxi, or US$2 by motorcycle taxi.

Pochentong Airport

By road

There are two points of entry by road, at Moc Bai on the Vietnamese border and Poipet on the Thai border. Usually the trip between Ho Chi Minh City and Phnom Penh takes five or six hours by taxi. If you are entering by this route make sure you already have a Cambodian visa and that your Vietnamese visa states clearly that Moc Bai is your exit point. You will be turned back if this is not the case.

Cambodian visas are obtainable at the Thai-Cambodia border but the grasping Cambodian officials are notorious for levying 'fines' on tourists. It's probably better to get your visa at the Cambodian embassy in Bangkok. At the moment this is not a good way to enter as the roads leading to both Siem Reap and Battambang are in dreadful condition.

By sea

Speedboats travel between Ban Had Lek in Trat Province, Thailand, and Koh Kong Town. You will need to have collected your Cambodian visa in Bangkok before embarking on this option. From Koh Kong there are boats leaving twice daily for Sihanoukville (Kompông Som).

Local bus near Kompông Cham

Getting Around

By plane

Siem Reap Airways, President Airlines and Phnom Penh Airways fly to Siem Reap and other cities in Cambodia. Keep in mind that routes and timetables change with frequency. Domestic airport tax is levied.

By bus

There are three air-conditioned bus services offering comfortable trips between Phnom Penh and Sihanoukville (Kompông Som). The road to Sihanoukville is the best in the country. There are buses to Siem Reap, but as the road is still in poor condition it is a long and tedious journey. For shorter trips, to say Oudong or Kompông Chhnâng, there are air-conditioned buses and these roads are in better condition than those further upcountry.

Phnom Penh railway station

By train

Train travel in Cambodia is to be avoided. The rolling stock is old, slow and uncomfortable. Trains to Sihanoukville (Kompông Som) and Kâmpôt run every other day and the journey takes approximately six hours. The other route runs to Battambang and also leaves Phnom Penh every other day. It takes 10 hours. Foreigners are not usually allowed to buy tickets for the Phnom Penh to Battambang route.

Speed guaranteed

By boat

Modern boats now ply the routes between Phnom Penh and Siem Reap, and Phnom Penh and Stung Treng. Boats for Siem Reap depart just beyond the Japanese Bridge at the northern end of Phnom Penh. Travelling up the Sap

river you will pass Cham fishing communities and as the boat enters Tonlé Sap large Vietnamese and Khmer boat communities can be seen. The journey takes around six hours. There is a daily boat to Kompông Cham with a journey time of two hours.

Taxis

Taxis are available at Pochentong airport, but they can be difficult to locate quickly in Phnom Penh. For trips in the capital expect to pay US$5 an hour. Outside the city the price is negotiable. There are plenty of taxis ready and willing to take you around the temples at Angkor. At the time of writing they charge US$20 a day in and around Angkor and Siem Reap. You will have to pay double that to visit the temples further afield, such as Bantay Srei. An option for long-distance travel is a shared taxi. These vehicles ply the routes between Phnom Penh and all the major towns. The drivers will usually wait until they have filled the vehicle to overflowing, so this is not always a comfortable form of transport, although it is certainly a cheap way to get around.

Long-distance taxi

Motorcycle taxis

Motorcycle taxis, or 'motos' as they are known, can be found all over the country. The drivers are usually recognisable by the fact that they wear a hat of some sort (crash helmets are not compulsory in Cambodia); the motorbikes also have larger seats than usual. Because taxis are sometimes hard to find in Phnom Penh the moto is the best way to get somewhere quickly. Many of the drivers speak some English. Always agree the fare beforehand, and remember to hold on tight as there are lots of potholes in the roads. Motos wait at the airport and this can be a viable way into town if you arrive alone.

'Motos' are common

Rental

Hotels and travel agents can arrange cars with drivers. It is still not possible to rent your own vehicle, which is probably a good thing as Cambodia's roads are dangerous. Motorbike rental is now becoming possible outside Phnom Penh. In Siem Reap certain cafés rent bicycles for a reasonable daily rate; in Phnom Penh the charge per day is slightly less.

Local public transport

In Phnom Penh the 'cyclo' (pedicab) can be seen on every street corner. They cost a little less than a moto, but are not as quick. The cyclo has three wheels and the driver sits behind you. Cyclos can be hired by the hour or by the day and are a great way to see the sights (except for Angkor). Agree a price before you go anywhere.

'Cyclo' at Central Market

Facts for the Visitor

Visas

For those arriving by air visas are available for most nationalities at Pochentong and Siem Reap airports. You need one black and white or colour passport picture and US$20. This is valid for 30 days. Tourist visas valid for 30 days can also be obtained through the Cambodian Embassy or Consulate in your own country. If you are entering the country from Vietnam then a visa must be obtained in Ho Chi Minh City. The Vietnamese entry point is Moc Bai and this should be clearly stamped on your Vietnamese visa if you wish to enter Cambodia via this route.

If you are planning to stay longer extensions are granted at the immigration office situated at No. 5, 200 Street (tel: 023-424 794). A 30-day extension costs US$30. Some travel agencies in Phnom Penh will handle extensions for a nominal fee.

Customs

French influence persists

The duty-free allowance for each visitor is one bottle of spirits and 200 cigarettes and a reasonable amount of perfume. If you are bringing a lot of video or photographic equipment make a list of it before you arrive at the customs declaration counter and be ready to show the customs officials. Hold on to this list for your departure.

Tourist information

There are no Cambodian tourist offices abroad and few embassies. There are, however, quite a few useful sites on the Internet: www.cambodia-web.net (the official site of the Cambodian Tourist Board); www.asiatour.com (very useful for helping plan your trip); www.camweb.org (general information on all things Khmer).

For visa information contact one of the following diplomatic representatives. Australia: 5 Canterbury Court, Deakin, Canberra, tel: 273 1259, fax: 272 1053; Japan: 8-6-9 Akasaka, Minato-ku, 107 Tokyo, tel: 3478 0861, fax: 3478 0865; Thailand: 185 Rajadamri Road, Bangkok, tel: 254 6630, fax: 253 9859; USA: 4500-16th Street, NW, 20011 Washington DC, tel: 726 7742, fax: 726 8381; Vietnam: 71 Tran Hung Dao Street, Hanoi, tel: 825 3788, fax: 826 5225.

Most transactions are made in dollars

Currency and exchange

The Cambodian currency is called the riel, although you will have little use for it. Almost all transactions in Phnom Penh, Sihanoukville (Kompông Som) and Siem Reap are made in US dollars. Notes come in denominations of 100,000, 50,000, 20,000, 10,000, 5,000, 2,000, 1,000, 500, 200 and 100. The import and export of riel is prohibited.

Ferry across the Mekong at Kompông Cham

It is a good idea to make sure you have plenty of small-denomination US dollars, as they are far easier to change than the larger notes.

Traveller's cheques have become easier to cash, as long as one is in well-touristed areas such as Phnom Penh, Siem Reap and Sihanoukville. Again it is preferable to have US dollar cheques. Credit cards have also become more widely accepted in Cambodia. Most decent hotels will accept Visa and MasterCard when paying hotel or restaurant bills. Cash advances on cards are possible in certain banks in Phnom Penh, Siem Reap, Battambang and Sihanoukville.

Tipping
Tipping is not a traditional part of Khmer culture, but with wages being so low it is appreciated. If you feel you have been well treated a small token of your gratitude would not be out of place. Hotels and top restaurants will have already added a service charge to your bill.

Time
Cambodia is seven hours ahead of Greenwich Mean Time (GMT). Cambodia is in the same time zone as Thailand and Vietnam.

Electricity
Electricity is rated at 220 volts. Power cuts do occur in Phnom Penh and just about everywhere else, although the government is doing its best to improve this situation. It is a good idea to carry a torch.

Opening times
Banks: Monday to Friday 8.30am–3.30pm.
Government offices and official bodies: Monday to Saturday 7.30am–11.30am and 2pm–5.30pm.
Post offices: Monday to Saturday 7am–7pm.

89

Floating restaurant at Tonlé Sap

General Post Office, Phnom Penh

Supermarkets: there are a number of places in Phnom Penh offering western food items. Lucky Market on Sihanouk Boulevard is probably the best.

National Museum: Tuesday to Sunday 8am–11.30am and 2.30pm–5.30pm.

Temples: generally daily 7am–5pm.

Banks, administrative offices and museums are closed on public holidays and occasionally on religious festivals.

Public holidays

These days are observed as official public holidays: 1 January (New Year's Day); 7 January (National Day); 8 March (International Women's Day); 13, 14, 15 April (Cambodian New Year); 1 May (International Workers' Day); May full moon (*Visakha Bochea*); May (Royal Ploughing Ceremony); 1 June (International Children's Day); 18 June (HM the Queen's Birthday); 24 September (Constitution and Coronation Day); September/October (*Prachum Ben*); 31 October (HM the King's Birthday); 9 November (Independence Day); November (Water Festival); 10 December (Human Rights Day). Chinese and Vietnamese New Year in January/February is not officially recognised as a holiday, but you will find some shops in Phnom Penh closed for a few days.

Phone box in Phnom Penh

Telephone and fax

Telephone boxes have been installed around Phnom Penh and other major tourist destinations. Many of these boxes take phone cards, and it is possible to telephone most countries directly. Cards for US$2, $5, $20, $50 and $100 can be purchased at the central Post Office in Phnom Penh and various hotels.

Etiquette

As in other Buddhist countries remember to remove your shoes when entering a private house or a temple. Keeping calm in tense situations is most important; Cambodians do not take kindly to someone losing their temper. The only thing anger achieves is more frustration.

Inside Wat Phnom

Beware of touching someone on the head – Cambodians believe one's vital essence resides in the head and therefore even a hairdresser will always ask permission before touching.

Equipment and luggage

A first-aid kit for the journey should include medicines for colds, diarrhoea and upset stomach as well as adhesive plasters, insect repellent and disinfectant. A small bag is useful for daily sightseeing either in Phnom Penh or at Angkor, preferably a small rucksack that you can put on your back.

Clothing

Cambodia is hot all year round, so it is unnecessary to bring a lot of heavy clothes. During the monsoon season things get pretty wet so do remember to bring along some light-weight protection against the rain. A strong pair of shoes is essential if you are visiting the temples at Angkor. You will find yourself doing a lot of clambering about. A hat is also recommended when visiting Angkor, as much of the site is exposed and it is amazing how quickly you can feel debilitated without something covering the head. Visiting one of Phnom Penh or Siem Reap's more exclusive restaurants will require reasonably smart clothes. If you do forget anything you will almost certainly be able to pick it up in Phnom Penh at one of the many markets.

Photography

Film is readily available in Phnom Penh. Agfa and Kodak print films and Fuji slide films are all on sale and there are plenty of places to get these films processed, although quality varies. Video film is also available.

Cambodians are usually quiet, polite people and on the whole do not mind being photographed, although it is always advisable to ask first. Show restraint when photographing people at prayer and monks. Also be careful when photographing soldiers or anything military.

Such pharmacy signs are common

Medical services

Good hospitals in Cambodia are few and far between and only a limited range of medicines are available. Minor ailments can be treated, but for anything major it would be best to get to Bangkok. The best hospitals in Phnom Penh in an emergency are Sos International Medical Centre, Street 51, tel: 023-216 911; Calmette Hospital, Monivong Boulevard, tel: 023-725 373. The Calmette is the largest hospital in Phnom Penh and has some French staff. The best pharmacy in Phnom Penh is the Pharmacie de la Gare, near the railway station, recommended for all medicines.

Health precautions

Immunisation is recommended for cholera, typhoid, tetanus and hepatitis.

Always drink bottled water, which is widely available, never tap water.

Malarial mosquitoes are widespread in the countryside, but as long as you are staying close to the tourist areas there should be no real problems. Nevertheless, it is advisable to bring along some good mosquito repellent for use on exposed skin at night. After dark it is advisable to wear long-sleeved shirts and long trousers. Consult your doctor about any recent advances in the treatment of malaria.

Seeking subjects

Beware of land mines

Police HQ in Phnom Penh

Take a taxi back to the hotel

Health insurance

It is recommended that travellers arrange comprehensive overseas travel sickness insurance, including transport home if necessary.

When travelling

It has become a lot easier and safer to travel in Cambodia, but precautions still need to be taken. It is not advisable to travel in the countryside after dark. In fact, it is best to be safely at your destination before the sun goes down. Visitors should follow some basic common-sense rules:

- Do not draw attention to your money
- Do not wear revealing clothing
- Do not try to hitchhike
- Do not wander about Phnom Penh and other cities alone at night
- Do not hesitate to tell a speeding driver to slow down
- Always try to let relatives or friends know where you are going and when
- In rural areas take heed of land mine notices. It will take years until all mines are cleared.

Crime

Phnom Penh used to be quite a dangerous city to move around in at night, but stricter policing has made it a lot safer. However, there have been a few incidents of robbery involving visitors. All have occurred late at night and usually while travelling on the back of a motorcycle taxi or moto. The lesson is to take a proper taxi back to your hotel late at night. In the unlikely event that you should be stopped by a robber, assume he may be armed and hand over whatever valuables you may be carrying.

Diplomatic representation

Australia and Canada: 11, 254 Street, Phnom Penh, tel: 023-213 470, fax: 023-213 413.

Japan: 75 Norodom Boulevard, Phnom Penh, tel: 023-217 161, fax: 023-217 162.

Laos: 15–17 Mao Tse Tung Boulevard, Phnom Penh, tel: 023-426 441, fax: 023-427 454.

Malaysia: 161, 51 Street, Phnom Penh, tel: 023-216 176, fax: 023-216 004.

Singapore: 92 Street and Norodom Boulevard, Phnom Penh, tel: 023-213 663.

Thailand: 4 Monivong Boulevard, Phnom Penh, tel: 023-426 182.

United Kingdom: 27–29, 75 Street, Phnom Penh, tel: 023-427 124, fax: 023-428 295.

United States of America: 27, 240 Street, Phnom Penh, tel: 023-216 436, fax: 023-216 437.

Accommodation

Good accommodation in Cambodia is limited to a few major centres: Phnom Penh, Siem Reap, Sihanoukville (Kompông Som) and Battambang. Phnom Penh offers a choice of luxury accommodation at very reasonable prices, considering what amenities are available. Mid-level accommodation can be found in abundance and is usually quite comfortable. At the lower end, guesthouses are now becoming more and more common and some of them are excellent. Compared to what was available a few years ago the general situation in Cambodia has improved tremendously. Above the US$20 point all rooms will be air-conditioned and normally have satellite television and a refrigerator. Hot water is usually available even in the cheaper guesthouses.

Listed below are hotel recommendations for some of the destinations covered in this book. They fall into the following price categories: $$$ = expensive; $$ = moderate; $ = inexpensive

Phnom Penh
Hotel Le Royal, 92 Rukhak Vithei Duan Penh (off Manivong Boulevard), tel: 023-981 888, fax: 023-981 168. A luxury hotel with a history. It has seen a succession of foreign guests, including all the top journalists of the Vietnam War. A tasteful renovation by the Raffles Group has made Le Royal the most exclusive hotel in town. $$$. **Hotel Cambodiana**, 313 Sisowath Quay, tel: 023-426 288, fax: 023-426 292, e-mail: luxury@hotelcambodiana.com.kh.

Hotel Cambodiana

A splendid hotel overlooking the confluence of the Sap, Bassac and Mekong rivers. It contains all the amenities of a modern hotel. $$$. **Inter-Continental**, 84 Manivong Boulevard (one block east of Manivong), tel: 023-424 888, fax: 023-424 885, e-mail: phnompenh@interconti.com. A five-star hotel with all the facilities of this worldwide chain. $$$. **Foreign Correspondents Club of Cambodia**, 363 Sisowath Quay, tel: 023-724 014. A floor below the renowned restaurant and bar, the FCCC has three well-appointed rooms with verandas overlooking the river. $$. **Sunway**, No.1, Street 92, Sangkat Wat Phanom, tel: 023-430 333, fax: 023-430 339. Newish business hotel in the same leafy neighbourhood as Hotel Le Royal. $$$. **Juliana Hotel**, 16, Street 152, Sangkat Veal Vong, tel and fax: 023-880 530. Away from the city centre, with health club, sauna and a good pool. The Juliana regards itself as Phnom Penh's premier business hotel. $$$. **Diamond Hotel**, 172–184 Manivong Boulevard, tel: 023-216 636, fax: 023-216 635. Centrally located in Phnom Penh's commercial district. $$. **Goldiana Hotel**, 10–12, 280 Street, tel: 023-723 085. An excellent mid-range hotel.

Very popular with non-governmental organisation staff (NGOs) and consultants. $$. **Holiday International**, 84 Manivong Boulevard, tel: 023-427 402, fax: 023-427 401. A 24-hour coffee shop, sauna and M2 Club disco. $$. **Renakse Hotel**, 40 Sothearos Boulevard, tel: 023-722 457, fax: 023-428 785. Beautiful French colonial-style hotel superbly located opposite the Royal Palace and very close to the riverfront. $$. **Sharaton Cambodia Hotel**, Street 47, near Wat Phnom Penh, tel: 023-360 395, fax: 023-360 393. Well located for visiting Wat Phanom and the Sap riverfront. $$. **Tai Ming Plaza Hotel**, 281 Norodom Boulevard, tel: 023-427 249, fax: 023-363 010. A modern Chinese-style hotel with Chinese restaurant and karaoke lounge. $$. **Beauty Inn**, 100 Sihanouk Boulevard, tel: 023-721 676, fax: 023-722 677. Situated in the heart of the business and commercial district. $. **Mittapheap Hotel**, 262 Manivong Boulevard, tel: 023-723 999, fax: 023-426 492. Cheap but clean hotel in the business district. $. **Walka-bout Hotel**, 109G, corner of Street 51 and Street 174. This popular mid-range place has a 24-hour restaurant. $$.

Grand Hotel D'Angkor

Siem Reap

Grand Hotel D'Angkor, 1 Vithei Charles de Gaulle, tel: 063-963 888, fax: 063-963 168, e-mail: grandhotel@raffles.com. This fabulous hotel is located in the centre of Siem Reap opposite King Sihanouk's villa. It was completely refurbished by the Raffles Group and can rightly claim to be one of Southeast Asia's grandest hotels. $$$. **Angkor Hotel**, Street 6, Phum Sala Kanseng, tel: 063-964 301, fax: 063-964 302. One of the better hotels in Siem Reap with an excellent restaurant and large swimming pool. $$. **Angkor Village**, Wat Bo Road, tel: 063-963 561, fax: 063-380 363. This hotel has a nightly performance of traditional apsara dance. $$. **Banteay Srei Hotel**, Street 6, Airport Road, tel/fax: 063-913 839. Represents good value for the amenities on offer. $$. **Bayon Hotel**, Phoum Wat Bo, Sangkat 4, tel: 063-631 769, fax: 063-963 993. Great location in the heart of Siem Reap old town, next to the small winding river. $$. **Golden Banana**, Wat Damnak, tel: 012-885 366. A newish collection of comfortable bungalows in a quiet neighbourhood. $. **Ta Phrom Hotel**, near Old Market, tel: 063-380 117, fax: 063-380 116. Very well situated next to the river, in the Old French quarter. $$. **Freedom Hotel**, Highway 6, near Central Market, tel: 063-963 473, fax: 063-964 274. There is a good restaurant attached to the hotel. $. **Ivy Guesthouse**, near the Old Market, tel: 063-800 860. Good place for local information, there is also a good bar attached. $. **Red Piano**, near the Old Market, tel: 012-854 150. Comfortable and stylish, this place has rooms with small verandas. Good restaurant and bar on the ground floor. $$.

On the farm near Kampôt

Battambang

Angkor Hotel, Street No.1, tel: 012-845 761. Overlooks the Sangker River, not far from the footbridge. $. **Chaya Hotel**, tel: 012-733 204. Popular budget accommodation in a shophouse building. $. **Teo Hotel**, tel: 012-857 048. Battambang's best value accommodation. Rooms were recently renovated and are clean and comfortable. $$.

Sihanoukville (Kampong Som)

CCS Hotel, Ekareach Street, tel: 034-933 720. Located near the centre of Sihanoukville and not far from Ochatial Beach. Apart from the hotel, CCS also has some very good bungalows on offer. $$. **Seaside Hotel**, 4th Quarter, Khan Mittapheap, Ochatial, tel: 034-933 641, fax: 034-640. No longer the largest but still probably the best hotel on Ochatial Beach. $$. **Chez Mari-Yan** Bungalows, Sangkat 3, Khan Mittapheap, tel: 034-916 468. Small but comfortable bungalows with verandas and a view of the sea. $. **Marlin Hotel**, Ekareach Street, tel: 034-320 169. Well managed with a good restaurant and bar attached. $. **Mealy Chenda Guesthouse**, Mondul 3, Sangkat 3, Khan Mittapheap, tel: 034-933 472. This large, long-running guesthouse overlooks Victory Beach. $. **King Gold Hotel**, Boray Kamakor Street, tel: 034-815 708. Popular midrange place with swimming pool and spa. $$. **Peak Hotel**, Near the port, tel: 034-320 301, fax: 034-320 300. A favourite with visiting high rollers, the Peak has a casino and helicopter pad, as well as tennis courts and a pool. $$$.

In the French Quarter in Kompông Cham

Kampot

Bokor Mountain Club, on the riverfront, tel: 033-932 314. Kampot's best accommodation choice in a tastefully restored colonial. $$. **Kampot Guesthouse**, tel: 033-885 255. Clean and comfortable budget accommodation with a good restaurant attached. $.

Index

© APA Publications GmbH & Co. Verlag KG Singapore Branch, Singapore.